Workday Gold: A Collection of Keith Bitikofer's #WorkdayTips Focused on Software Functionality 2021-2023

Keith Bitikofer

Published by Keith Bitikofer, 2024.

While every precaution has been taken in the preparation of this book, the publisher assumes no responsibility for errors or omissions, or for damages resulting from the use of the information contained herein.

WORKDAY GOLD: A COLLECTION OF KEITH BITIKOFER'S #WORKDAYTIPS FOCUSED ON SOFTWARE FUNCTIONALITY 2021-2023

Table of Contents

Dear Friend,

What started as an experiment grew beyond anything I would've ever expected. In the past two years, my posts have grown to over 1.5 million views. It has been amazing to have my posts impact and encourage so many people in their Workday© journey.

I've even had interactions at Workday Rising and other events, where many people have said, "Oh, you're Keith from LinkedIn!".

My posts include tips about Workday functionality as well as general Workday support team suggestions. I recognize that many people don't have time to go back through all of my old posts (which can be difficult on LinkedIn), even though many of my Workday functionality posts are still just as valuable and valid to this day.

At a recent event, someone thanked me for all the posts I have done over the years. This person went on to say that not only have they updated their Workday tenant based on suggestions from my posts, but they are sure that hundreds of companies have done the same thing. That was not only humbling to hear, but also quite encouraging, and it led me to the idea of creating this eBook.

This conversation made me realize that I really wanted to find an easy way to share all of my Workday functionality-related posts in one easy-to-read location. I went back through every post I've made for the last two years and assembled all of the software functionality posts. I've taken the time to organize them into categories and into comprehensive lists so that others could have all of them in one place.

I'm also working on additional Workday-related books. So be sure to look for them in the future. Until then, I hope you find this helpful!

Sincerely,

Keith Bitikofer

Suggestions on How to
Best Leverage this Book

There are 50+ posts in this eBook, which can seem a bit overwhelming when you don't know where to start.

Start with the topics that most interest you! Thankfully, you do not need to worry about reading the content in chronological order. In fact, in order to best utilize this resource, I'd suggest that you pick a chapter that you are most interested in and dive into that topic.

Check out the comments on the actual LinkedIn posts. Each post in this eBook is just the beginning of what you can learn about each topic. A lot of my LinkedIn followers have also found their own helpful ways to leverage Workday, and oftentimes, they gracefully share their experiences in the comment section. I've included the links to the original posts to make it easier for you to check out these comments. Feel free to add additional comments for others to see as well! In those comments, you will find references and possibly see questions you never thought to ask, being answered for you.

Enjoy! Thanks for joining me on this journey!

About the Author

From 2014-2020, Keith was a project manager, HRIS director, Enterprise Systems director, etc. at a large global nonprofit organization that used Workday. He was the project manager for the initial Workday HCM project, then led the teams that supported Workday as they rolled out the Financial Modules, a global rollout to around 40 of their partner organizations, Prism, many Extend apps, hundreds of integrations, etc.

As the footprint of this organization's use of Workday grew, their support team and support team model had to morph and grow with the needs. Based on this experience, plus a total of 30+ years of experience in IT and Operations roles in Higher Ed, Manufacturing, Consulting, and Nonprofit, he now helps coach the management and staff of other companies that use Workday and other software systems.

For the past few years, Keith has been a partner and consultant at EMD, which is an official Workday Partner. To find additional information on EMD, visit EnterpriseMarketDesk.com/

Mentoring/Coaching—Starting in 2020, he has been providing one-on-one coaching for Workday support teams and career coaching. If you are interested in learning more about this, please reach out to Keith to schedule a discovery call.

Keith would love to connect with you!

You can find him on LinkedIn at LinkedIn.com/in/Keith-Bitikofer

Sign up for his newsletter and learn more about how he work with people and see what others are saying about working with him: KeithBitikofer.com

Cross Platform Tips for End Users

Leverage multiple browser tabs!

November 2022

Right-click on any hyperlinked text and select 'open in new tab.' This allows you to have the report in one tab but research info about a Worker, Customer, Supplier, etc. in additional tabs. Then, you can go back to the tab with the report and don't have to rerun it each time.

Leverage multiple browsers!

January 2022

If you support Workday, you often want to or need to be logged into multiple Workday tenants at the same time. This way you can compare the Tenant configuration, reports, or integrations between different tenants.

By using multiple browsers, (i.e. Chrome, Safari, Firefox) you can be logged into separate tenants with each browser. With Chrome, you can also use 'incognito windows' or separate Chrome Profiles.

Consider always using the same browser for your access to your Prod tenant. This way you don't accidentally do a test in Prod!

For me, I use Chrome with multiple Chrome Profiles for all my testing and Safari for my Prod access.

Leverage Prefix Words in your Workday searches.

May 2022

For years I have used Prefix Words like 'bp:' or 'domain:' to start out my searches in Workday. However, I had no idea how many Prefix Words Workday has!

If you have the new 'Workday Today' homepage and search screens turned on, check this out:

Enter something in the Search bar, then click 'return' / enter on your keyboard (as opposed to using the drop-down).

This will take you to the search screen, with the categories down the left that you can use as filters.

At the lower left of the screen, you will see 'View Search Tips'. Click on it.

There are pages and pages of Prefix Words listed alphabetically. Depending on your role, different ones will be more helpful than others, but it is certainly worth scrolling through the list!

You can also type "?" in the search bar and hit enter so it takes you to the same results.

Leverage keyboard shortcuts!

November 2022

When you are entering a date in Workday, you don't have to key in the full year of the date. Just enter '22' for the year 2022 and tab to the next field. Then Workday will fill in the full year.

Now, I suspect that most of the people following me already knew that. However, I'm often surprised when I'm working with an end user and having them walk me through something they are doing in Workday and I see them entering the full year. Some have been using Workday for years and are delighted when I share this shortcut with them.

So, please make sure the end users you support know about all the shortcuts you use in Workday to make your life easier (such as using multiple browser tabs, etc).

Suggestions for drop-down lists:

- If you want to select everything in a multi-select list (before or after searching) then ctrl+A to select and space bar to select (or unselect).

- You can scroll down the list, hold shift, and click the lowest box in the area you want to select all the options above. Repeat to also untick.

- If you are searching in a very long selection prompt, you can press a letter to jump to that section of the list or type in part of the phrase in the list. For example, if you are searching for "United States of America" in a list, you can type "of am" and it pulls it up immediately.

Suggestions for date fields:

- Hitting the space bar on a calendar selection to automatically get today's date.

- When in a year's field, you can use the navigation up/down arrows on your keyboard for the near years.

Proxy Suggestions:

- Remember to use multiple browsers when you are proxying as different people for various testing.

- If you are testing as multiple different users in a row (that have different roles/security) and you are already proxied as someone, you can just do 'start proxy' to switch to the next person instead of doing 'stop proxy' and start proxy over again. In other words, you can skip the stop proxy step.

- You can also look up the person, then use the Related Actions to select 'start proxy'. This can be faster than doing the 'start proxy' task and looking up the person there.

Type '?' in the search bar to see the list of Prefixes you can search on. Or, if you have the new search functionality turned on, you can see the next section for a new way to see all the prefixes.

For direct links to each LinkedIn post, please visit
KeithBitikofer.com/Workday-Gold-SF-Links/

Security Tips

Leverage the 'Worker Security' report on the Worker Profile Page

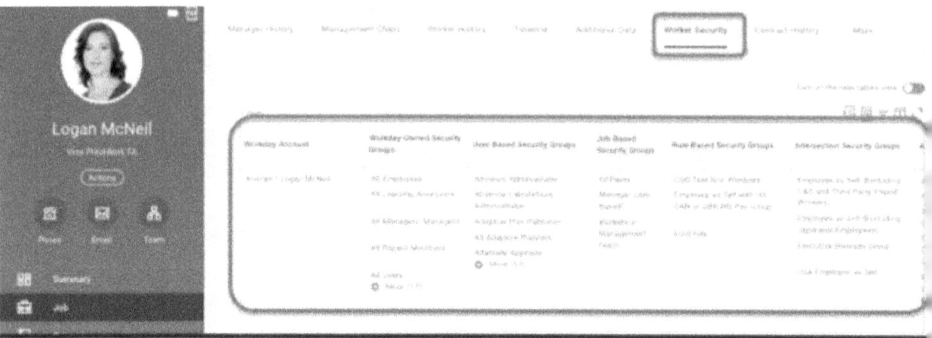

May 2022

For those of you who help troubleshoot security or worker access issues, the 'Worker Security' report can be incredibly helpful.

This is a relatively new option. So, depending on when you started using Workday, this may already be set up in your system. For customers that have been live on Workday for a while, I'd suggest you consider adding it to your Worker Profile page. The pictured screenshot is from the GMS tenant.

You can add this by the following steps (assuming you have config access to do this):

- Search on 'Configure Profile Group'
- Select 'Job for Worker Profile'
- Add 'Worker Security' to the list of reports/tabs

If the Worker Security report isn't available in your tenant, you can duplicate it from what is in the GMS tenant. If you don't have access to a GMS tenant, I have the report definition in an Excel file. This document is accessible via the link at the end of this chapter.

This is really useful to see all the different security groups (user-based, job-based, rule-based, etc.) that a specific user is in.

Be intentional about managing and maintaining your Workday security configuration!

August 2023

Who owns your Workday security configuration? For some of you, this will seem obvious. But, for companies new to Workday, there can be a lot of discussion about this.

There are two aspects to managing Workday Security:

1 - Who has the authority to decide what various roles or people have access to in Workday?

2 - Who makes the actual updates to security in your tenant?

1 - Who has the authority to decide what various roles or people have access to in Workday?

You should have some leadership-level person or team speaking into decisions about which positions/people have access to what data in Workday. This could be the CHRO or other HR leadership person or team, for the HCM data. Individuals may think they should have more access to data than is required for their position. With GDPR and state-specific data rules, it is more and more important to be intentional and wise about who has access to the more confidential data, such as social security numbers, compensation, etc.

2 - Who makes the actual updates to security in your tenant?

Are you going to have multiple people who can update security in your Production Tenant?

Or are you going to only have one (and a backup) person that makes changes in Production?

For me, I'd like to limit the number of people making changes in Production. This way, if there is an issue in Production, I (as a manager) only have to go to one person and ask what was changed that could have created the current issue.

If multiple people are making changes in Production (even if they are highly experienced consultants), it can be difficult to figure out who made the change that broke a given process in Workday.

For the Implementation tenants, it makes perfect sense to have other team members have access to making security changes. Then, once they have built out their changes and tested them, they can work with the Security Admin person to do the final migration to Production.

Where the Security Admin person sits in your overall structure is a whole additional question. They could be in HRIS, IT, or on a FIN support team.

Monitor Implementer and Service Center User Accounts

August 2023

Do you know who has access to your Workday tenant?

When was the last time you reviewed who has access to your Workday tenant and whether it is up to date?

As Workday customers, we are good at quickly removing system access when an employee leaves.

However, how quickly do you remove access when an implementation consultant no longer needs access to your tenants/system?

When you do a Workday project, you often work with consultants to help configure Workday, load data, etc. The implementation consultants get access to all your configuration setup AND all your data. This is necessary and appropriate during the project. However, many customers forget that it is the customer's responsibility to 'inactivate' those accounts once the project is done.

Another scenario is for ongoing post-production AMS / ticket support when a vendor sets up their consultants in the Workday Service Center (in your tenant) to access it. These consultants need to have ongoing access for them to support you well. However, as an example, one time I looked at our list and found a large group of consultants still active in our tenant that I knew no longer worked for that vendor. The vendor was supposed to be maintaining this list. But they had forgotten.

Recommendation: Don't just rely on the vendor to guard your system access.

How do you do this? Use the 'View Implementers' and 'View Service Center Users' standard reports. Use the related actions on a consultant in the list -> Security Profile -> Edit Workday Account.

Make sure that the 'Account Disabled' is set to 'yes' for those who shouldn't have access to your system. You can also add a date in the 'Account Expiration Date' field if you know when a project will end. You can always change the date or set the Account Disable to be 'no', if they come back to help with another project in the future.

Also, remember to disable access to any non-Prod/implementation tenants and Customer Central as well.

I'd suggest that you pick a date and put it on your annual calendar. It could be annually on Jan 1 or Jan 15. You could also do it quarterly.

Ask your vendors to give you a notification anytime a consultant leaves so that you can immediately disable access.

You could also set accounts to expire on Jan 1 or specific quarterly, semiannual or annual basis, for longer-term consultants. You may want to consider applying this policy to some of your contingent worker records as well.

For direct links to each LinkedIn post, please visit
KeithBitikofer.com/Workday-Gold-SF-Links/

Custom Report Tips

How many of your custom reports haven't been run in the last year?

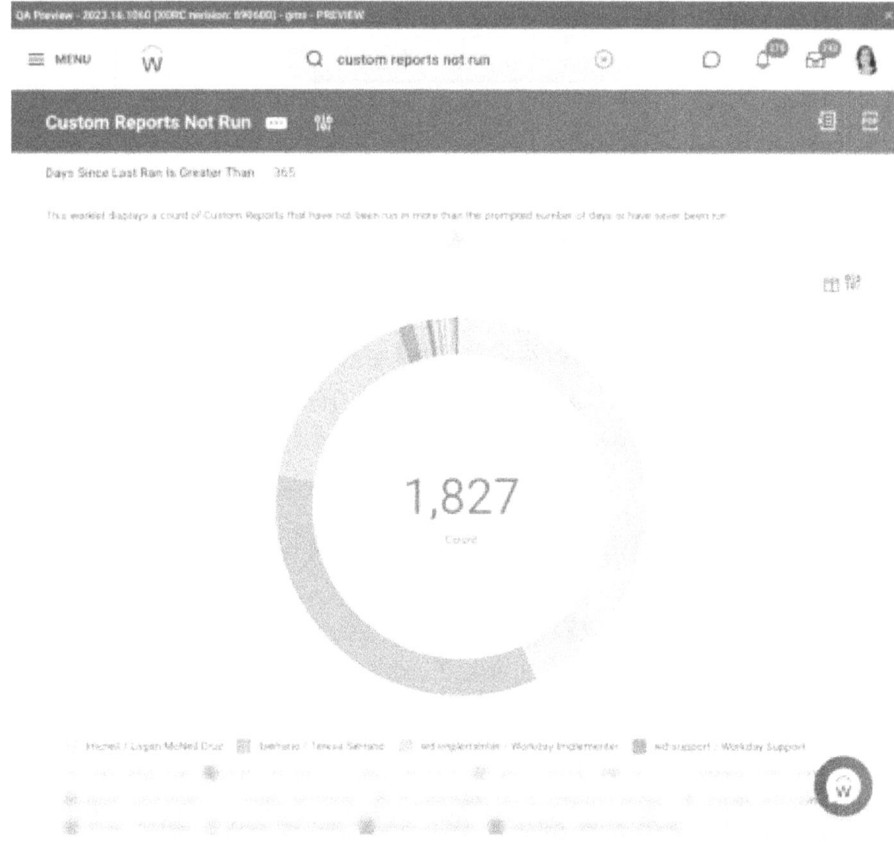

April 2023

Time for spring cleaning!

The longer you have been using Workday, the longer this list becomes!

Some reports are only used once a year, at year-end, or an annual basis. Please don't delete those! (Hint- add a report tag of 'Annual' for those so nobody deletes them accidentally!)

- Other reports were created and the owner left the company.

- Or they were created from some specific request by leadership, only to never be used again.

- Or maybe people just forgot it was out there!

The list goes on!

I encourage you to run the 'Custom Reports Not Run' report, which is also on the Report Administrator Dashboard, if you have that enabled. I'm guessing you will be surprised by the results!

I know of one customer with around 1900 reports listed on this report.

A common scenario for this is consultants that created audit reports during your implementation and nobody even knows they are there (may or may not be shared with anyone). You can 'transfer ownership' to yourself. Do a test run of it to see if it is anything useful. Then decide if you are just going to delete it or not.

How about you? How many reports are in your tenant that haven't been run in the last year? As a Workday customer, how does your team manage this list?

This could be a quarterly, semiannual, or annual review process.

Leverage 'Enable Save Parameters' on Custom Reports

July 2022

Anytime you have multiple prompts on a custom report or have a long list of options for one or more prompts (like the list of cost centers, projects, sup orgs), it can be super helpful to allow users to save the prompt values they selected, to make it easier to run the report next time.

It is very easy to add. When you edit a custom report, go to the Advanced tab and click the check box for 'Enable Save Parameters'.

For the 'Find Journals' or the 'Find Journal Lines' report, I often make a copy of the Workday delivered reports and at least default the company prompt to be the customer's primary company. Then I also enable the save parameters.

Make sure to also notify your heavy report users of this. I thought it would be obvious. But, for many users, they didn't even notice it. They got really excited once I explained it to them, but they wouldn't have noticed it otherwise.

Extra credit- Once it has been in use for a while- you can look at the 'Saved Filter Usages' under the Report Tags to see what filters users have created.

Create a 'report of reports' to list custom reports

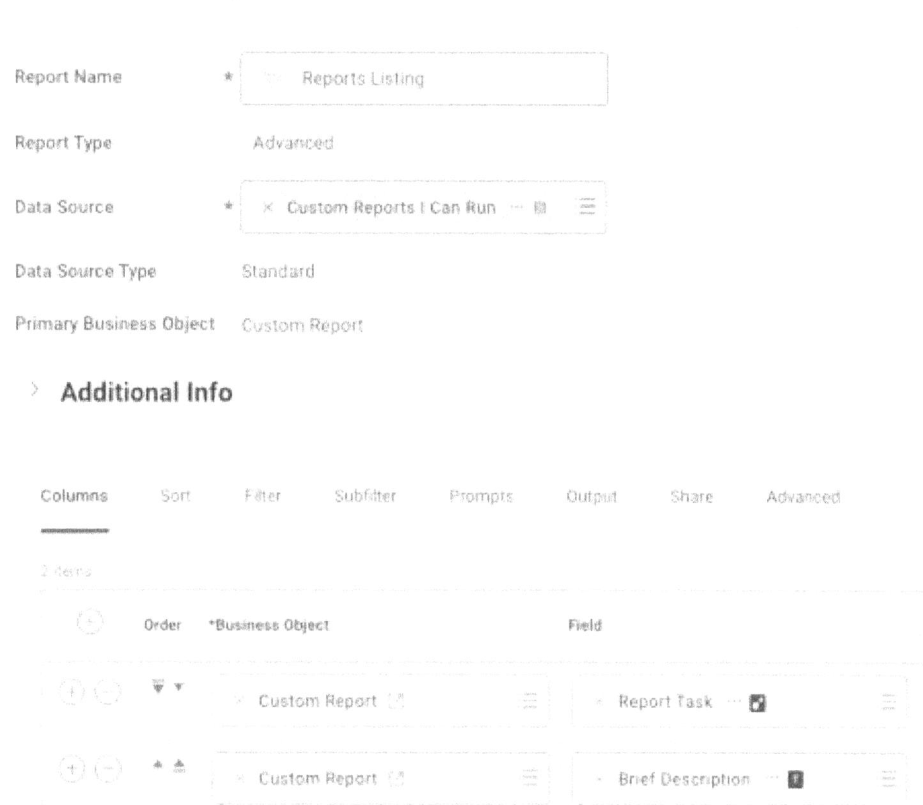

December 2021

Do your users keep forgetting about custom reports they asked for and that you created for them? Sometimes they forget the names of the reports you created and then don't know how to find them.

Solution? Create a 'report of reports' (using the 'Custom Reports I can Run' data object, filtered by report tags) that lists all the custom reports used by their department or type of user. The report names are hyperlinked, so you can just click it to run the report. Then add it to a custom Dashboard for their department. You can also include a short description of the purpose of each report, which is helpful for new staff.

See the section about Report Tags next.

Leverage Report Tags

January 2022

Report tags can be used for a variety of purposes:

- Tag reports with a department name or a specific user group that has reports unique to them. Then create a 'report of reports' filtering on that departmental report tag.

- Tag reports as 'integrations' or 'in testing'. Used to create reports listing all your integrations or reports used for integration. Or tracking reports that are currently in testing to get user feedback, etc.

- Tag reports as 'annual or semi-annual'. Sometimes when you are reviewing the reports that haven't been used for a while to delete old reports, you could accidentally delete key reports that are only used once a year. This tag can be a helpful reminder that while these reports aren't used much, they are still critical- and you definitely don't want to delete them!

Review / Delete Temporary Reports

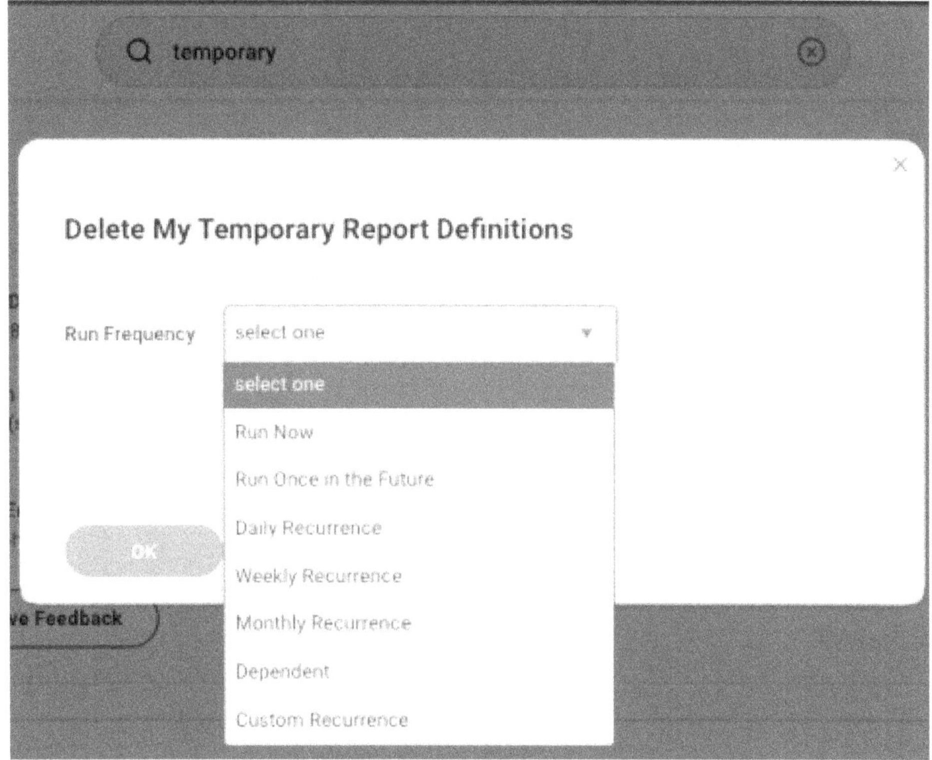

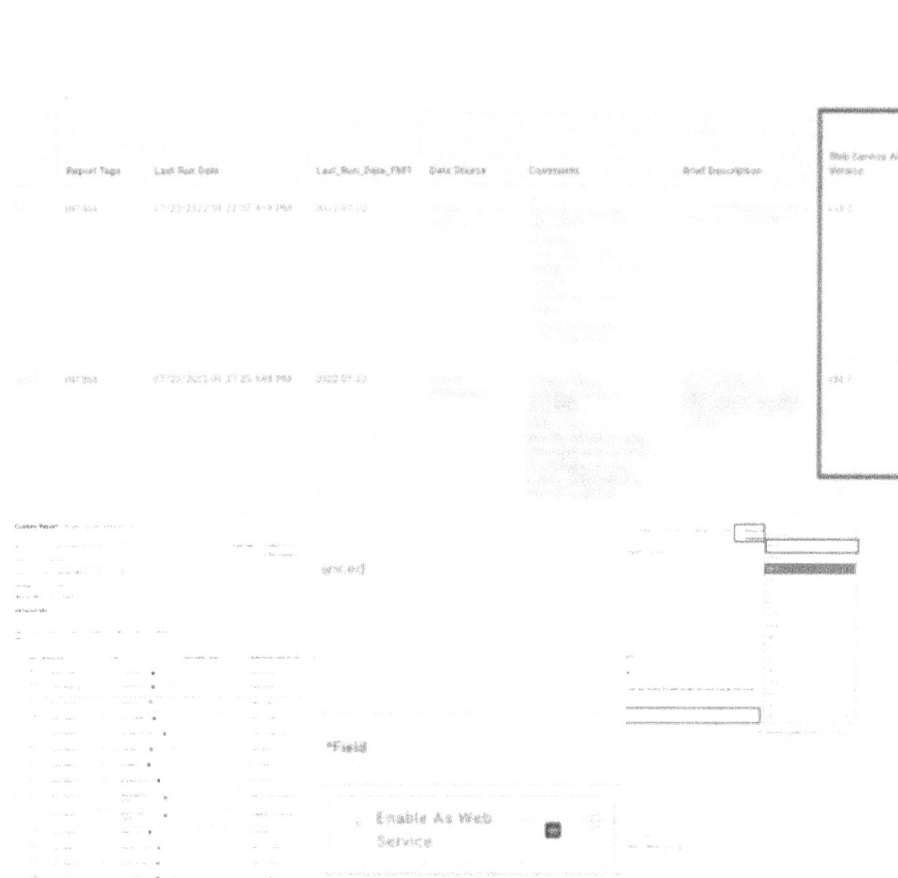

October 2022

In the past, Workday release versions were numbers (32,33, 34, etc.). Then they switched to 2022 R1, 2022 R2, etc. With each new release, there are data model changes. New fields are added and some other fields are removed or 'deprecated'. When Workday is in the process of removing fields, they will be marked as 'do not use'. I have heard that Workday typically gives 18 months before they actually remove access to a field.

Many integrations use custom reports that are web-enabled. (This includes Prism-enabled reports). These reports all have a specific version/data model that they were originally designed for, which still uses the old numbering. We are currently at version 39. Having a custom report tied to the specific version that it uses reduces the chance of issues when a new version comes out.

However, over time, these reports can become 'outdated' and need to be updated. To update them, you just go the the Advanced tab in the report writer and change the version in the 'Web Services API Version' drop-down.

HOWEVER- You must do this in an Implementation Tenant first! Test running the report and integrations that use that report BEFORE doing this in Production. While many times, everything will work fine, you won't know for sure until you TEST it!

I'd encourage you to review the list of web-enabled custom reports you have and the API version annually, to be sure that none of them are more than a year or two old. You can do this by using the sample report that I included in the screenshots.

Encourage users to use 'column preferences' option

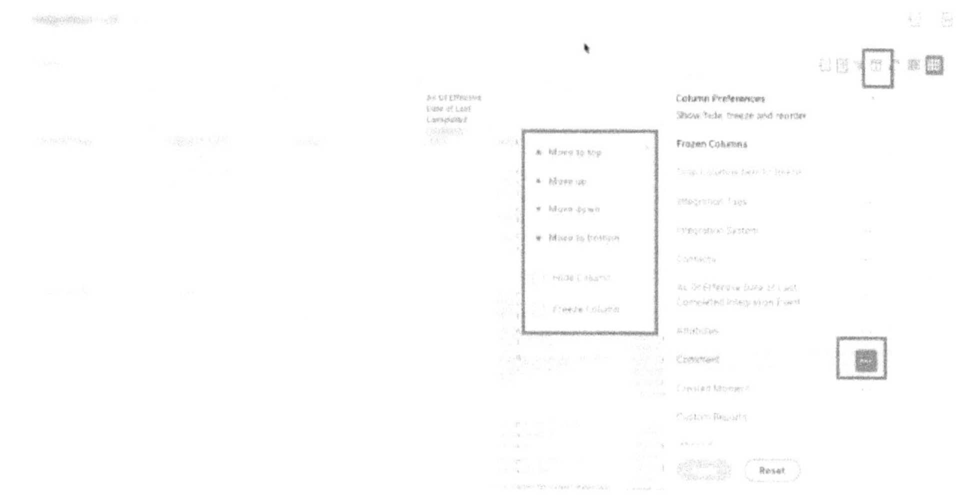

September 2022

Workday continues to add more preference options for users on Custom Reports. These are user-specific. So, as the report creator, you could create a report that multiple people/departments could use, even though they don't all want to see all the columns. Then show the users how to hide and reorder the columns to be the way they want to see them.

As a reminder, when you dump it into Excel, it ignores all the preference options that users have made (hiding or reordering columns). I have had some users complain about this, but it isn't as big of a deal if you warn them about it upfront.

It is a really helpful feature and, if you can get multiple users to use the same report with their own preferences this way, it may reduce the number of custom reports you need. It can also reduce the number of report change requests of 'Can you switch the order of these columns?'.

Notes:

- When you edit the report and add a new field, the new field(s) will appear at the end of the report if you have column preferences active. I kept looking for the new field where I added it to the report!

- If users start asking why a column they are supposed to see is missing - it can be because in "list/column mode" they have hidden those columns. Check this first, before thinking it is a security access issue, which we commonly have to troubleshoot.

There's also a great contributed solution on Workday Community for flexible reporting where you make the columns selectable in the report prompts. I've made this available via the link at the end of this chapter.

Leverage Matrix Reports!

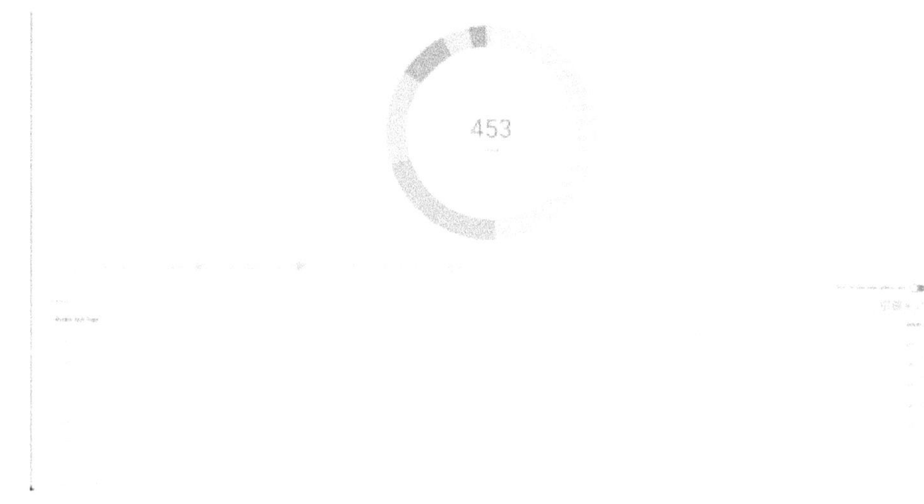

January 2022

Matrix reports allow you to quickly summarize Workday data. Examples include summarization of your company's hires or terminations- by worker type. Then you can include lots of drill-down options for users to see the details (based on their security).

The easiest way to learn how to create Matrix reports? Find ones you like in the GMS sample tenant and duplicate them in your own tenant!

Another idea is to start by creating an Advanced report to get the filters the way you want them, then create a Matrix report with the same filters.

Final suggestion: On your matrix report, scroll to the bottom right corner and click on the overall total to see all the detailed records the Matrix report is including in the summaries. We have had some users start to do that instead of using the Advanced reports that just had the detailed data.

Track the usage of your Dashboards in Workday!

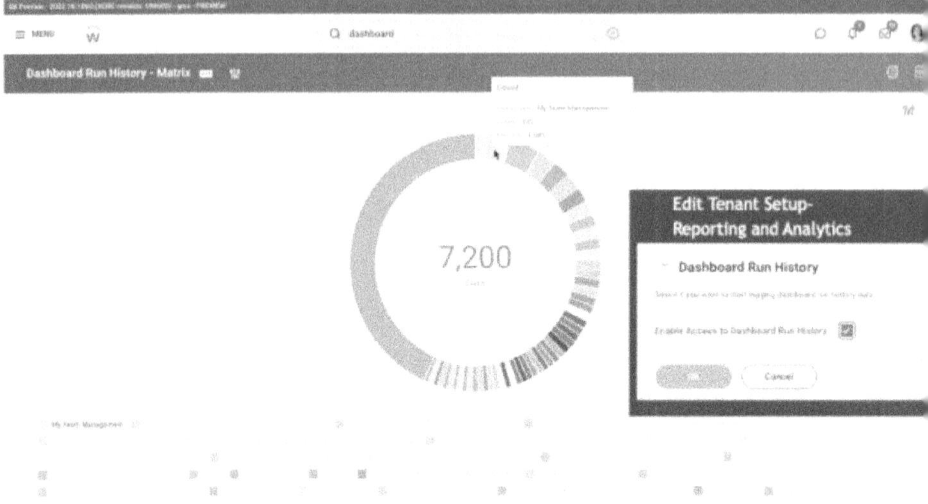

April 2023

Over the years we have spent many hours building lots of dashboards. The frustrating thing was that it was very hard to tell if anyone actually USED the dashboards based on all that hard work!

Now you CAN track that usage!

First, you have to go to 'Edit Tenant Setup - Reporting and Analytics' and click the check box to 'Enable Access to Dashboard Run History'.

From that point forward (and not before!) Workday will track the tenant-wide Dashboard usage/run history. Yea!

There is a standard matrix report called the 'Dashboard Run History' report in the GMS Tenant. The screenshot is of a copy of the report where I changed the output to show the 'Chart and Table'.

The data source is 'Indexed Dashboard Run History'.

Being able to track usage on the dashboards is also useful so that you can get rid of the ones that nobody is using anymore.

Leverage Workday Discovery boards

November 2022

Workday Discovery boards are another way to create reports in Workday. It uses a 'drag and drop' process to create new reports.

You can create a dashboard with multiple tabs and multiple visualizations on each tab. You can add at least 10 or more visualizations to a tab (vs the 6 you can add to a typical Workday dashboard). While it started with just charts, you can now also create visualizations that are rows and columns, like an advanced report.

Workday has a set of examples or 'Delivered Discovery Boards' that you can enable in your tenants to help you get started. (You have to enable the 'Discovery Boards: Managed Delivered Discovery Boards' domain.) If you have access to a GMS tenant, you can search on 'Delivered Discovery Boards' to see the list. Then you select one to view, copy it, and click the link to go to Drive to select and view it.

Check out the 'Discovery Boards' summary page in Community. It is a great list of resources to help you learn more about Discovery boards, videos, examples, instructions on how to enable it, etc.

Check out the Discovery Boards Guidance page in Community for more information. You can find this link via the link at the end of this chapter.

For direct links to each LinkedIn post, please visit
KeithBitikofer.com/Workday-Gold-SF-Links/

Preparing for New Workday Releases

Preparing for a new Release Webinar

Customer Perspective: Preparing for new Workday releases

January 2023

How do you prepare for a new Workday Release? Twice a year, Workday does a new release. This happens in March and September of every year. Workday gives us access to the new code 5 weeks in advance of the new release go-live date. There are often lots of webinars highlighting the new features around the time of new releases, but not many people talk about how to build a repeatable process from a customer perspective of how to get ready for new releases.

When we first went live with Workday, my goal was to have any new Workday Release be a 'non-event' to our users. I was always worried that we would get buried with new help desk tickets the week a new release came out, due to a major user interface change or something being broken. To reduce this stress, we implemented a standard process that we go through with each new release to make sure that we are prepared.

I have done a presentation called 'Preparing for a new release, from a customer perspective', which is available on Workday Community. This is based on the processes that we created at the customer that I worked for.

To access the recording, simply click on the link on the community page and 'register' for it. Then you will be able to watch the recording. The slides are also available in the comments section of this page.

Use the link a the end of this chapter to find the recording link on Workday Community, with a link to the slides in the comments section.

Run the 'All Custom Reports with 'Do Not Use' items' report!

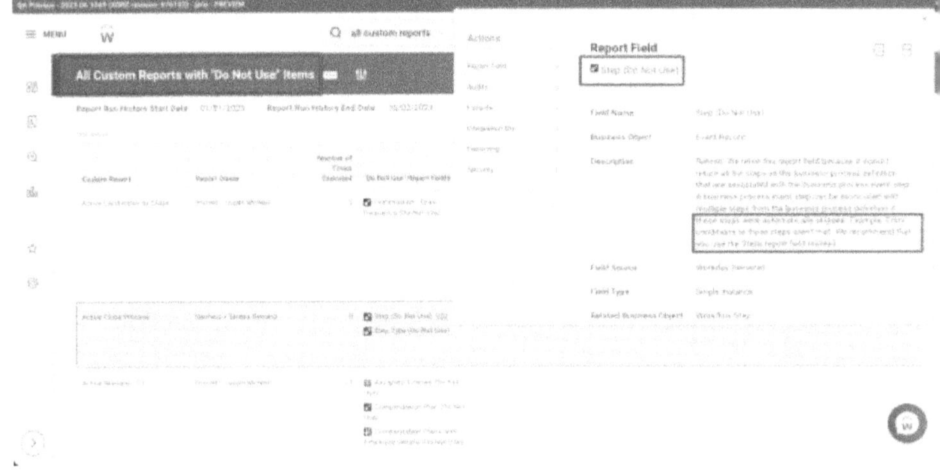

February 2023

Run the 'All Custom Reports with 'Do Not Use' items' report!

The 'Do Not Use' items/fields are any fields or business objects that Workday is deprecating in the new future. I've also called them 'DNU' fields for short.

The report tells you what fields need to be replaced. Before you even open the report to fix it, click on the related action three dots and look at the description. It usually tells you what field to use instead, such as switching to the 'Steps' report field on the screenshot for this post. This screenshot was taken from a GMS tenant.

Often it is easy to find and replace the old field with the new field. But sometimes the field isn't displayed on the report. It could also be in a filter or in a calc field used by the report. So, you may have to dig to find where the field is used on the report.

If it is in a calc field, be sure to look at the 'where used' to see all the reports that will be impacted by the change. Then test all of them after making the change.

Make the changes in Sandbox first and test them out before making the change in Prod.

In some cases, the report that needs to be fixed will be one used by an integration. After fixing the report, make sure to test the integration as well as just testing the report.

Allow plenty of time for this. Some will be easy to fix, but others will be more complicated than it appears at first. If a business object is being deprecated, you will have to build a whole new report, which obviously takes more time.

Be sure to assign someone on your team to own this cleanup process and schedule it to happen at least twice a year!

How about you? What best practices have you found with managing the 'Do Not Use' process of deprecating fields/objects in Workday?

Run the Audit Reports!

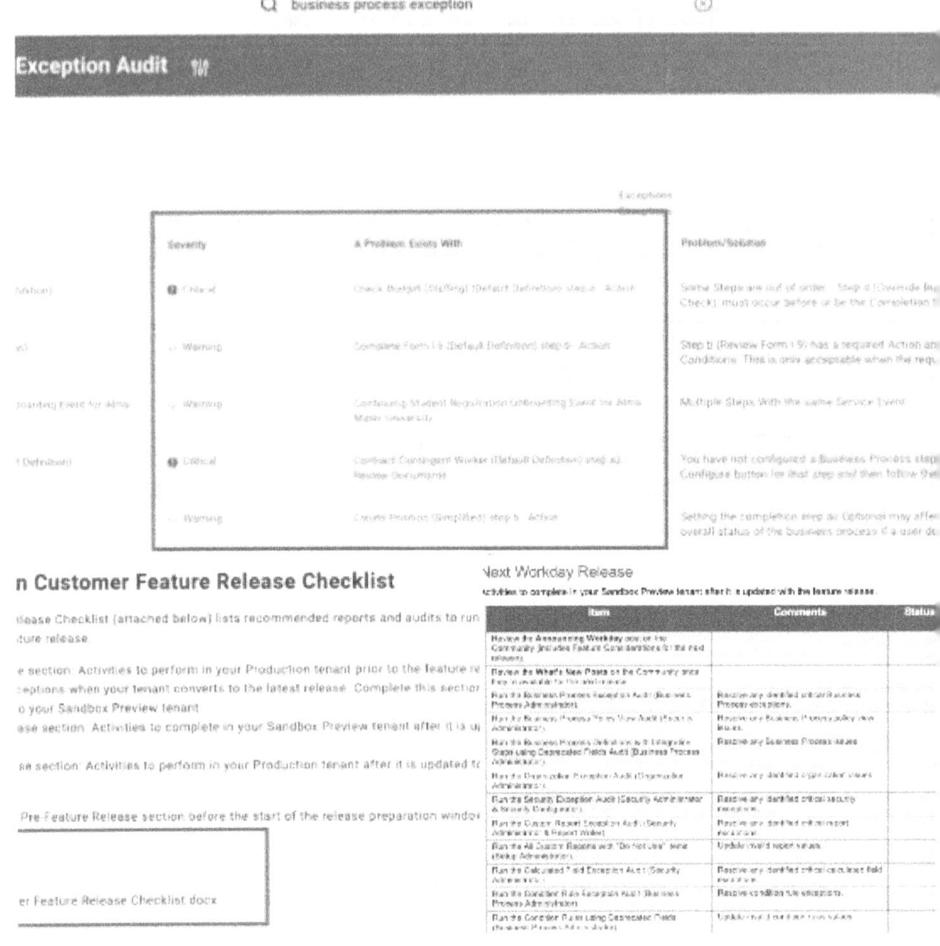

February 2023

I know everyone gets busy and focused on fighting whatever 'fires' (emails!) seem to be the highest priority or the easiest to knock out. But it is critical for you to be intentional about getting prepared for new releases.

A key thing to do is to run the recommended Audit Reports. Look for the 'Workday Customer Feature Release Checklist' doc at the End of the page below in Community. I included a sample screenshot of the latest listing of audit reports (from a GMS tenant).

The results of the audit reports give you detailed things to review and fix. Some are just warnings while others are 'critical' and need to be fixed.

It is all too easy to put these things off until your end users start coming to you with issues.

Be proactive instead!

**For direct links to each LinkedIn post, please visit
KeithBitikofer.com/Workday-Gold-SF-Links/**

Adjust Profile Pages

Adjust the 'Profile Header Card' on the Worker Profile (Part 1 of 4)

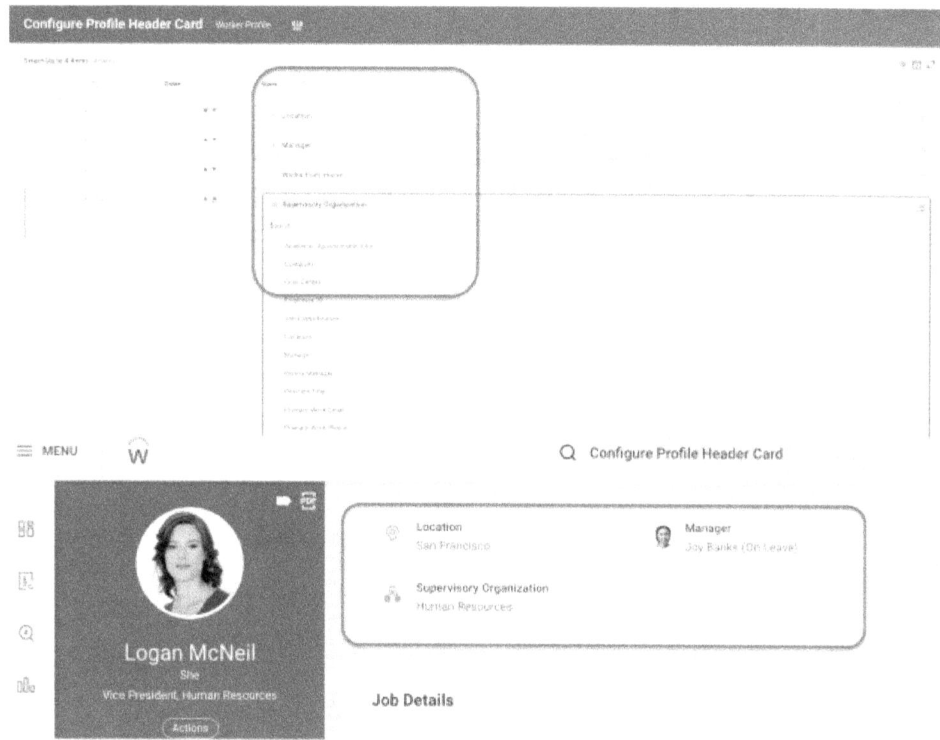

December 2022

On the Worker Profile page, the first 'card' that shows up is configurable. You can select from a list of data fields what will be most helpful to show on the summary page. New ones get added from time to time, such as the 'work from home'. Evaluate the ones you currently have listed. It is entirely possible that you have fields listed that you don't use anymore or don't add value to users anymore.

To edit this, use the 'Configure Profile Header Card' task

Select the 'worker profile' from the drop-down.

Then you can add, remove, or reorder the Data 'items' for the card.

In a test tenant, or the Shared Tenants in Community, you could test this out by adding and removing the various 'items' (max of 4) to see how they each look. Then decide which would be most helpful for your users.

You can also use the Configure Profile Header Card to update the summary section of other Profiles, such as Prospect, Candidate, and External Committee Member profiles.

Adjust Profile pages to match your users' needs! (Part 2 of 4)

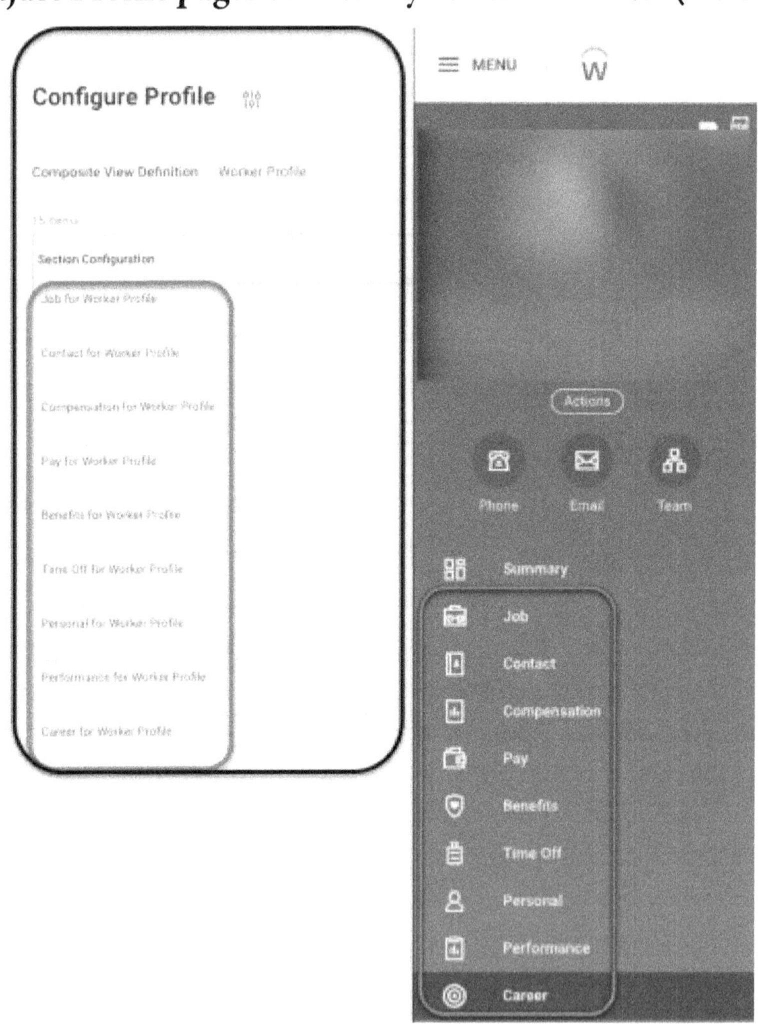

December 2022

Workday gives you the ability to configure the 'sections' in all the various 'profile' pages. There are 100+ 'profile' pages that you can select from to configure, depending on which modules you have. Profile pages include the main page for workers, companies, cost centers, etc.

You have the ability to turn sections on and off, and change the order of the sections (but you can't add your own to them). The one that most people would consider changing is probably the 'Worker Profile'.

Use the 'Configure Profile' task to check this out.

For many of you, these may still be the default configuration from when you started using Workday. Check them out in a test tenant or in a GMS tenant, if you have access to one.

Adjust Profile pages to match your users' needs! (Part 3 of 4)

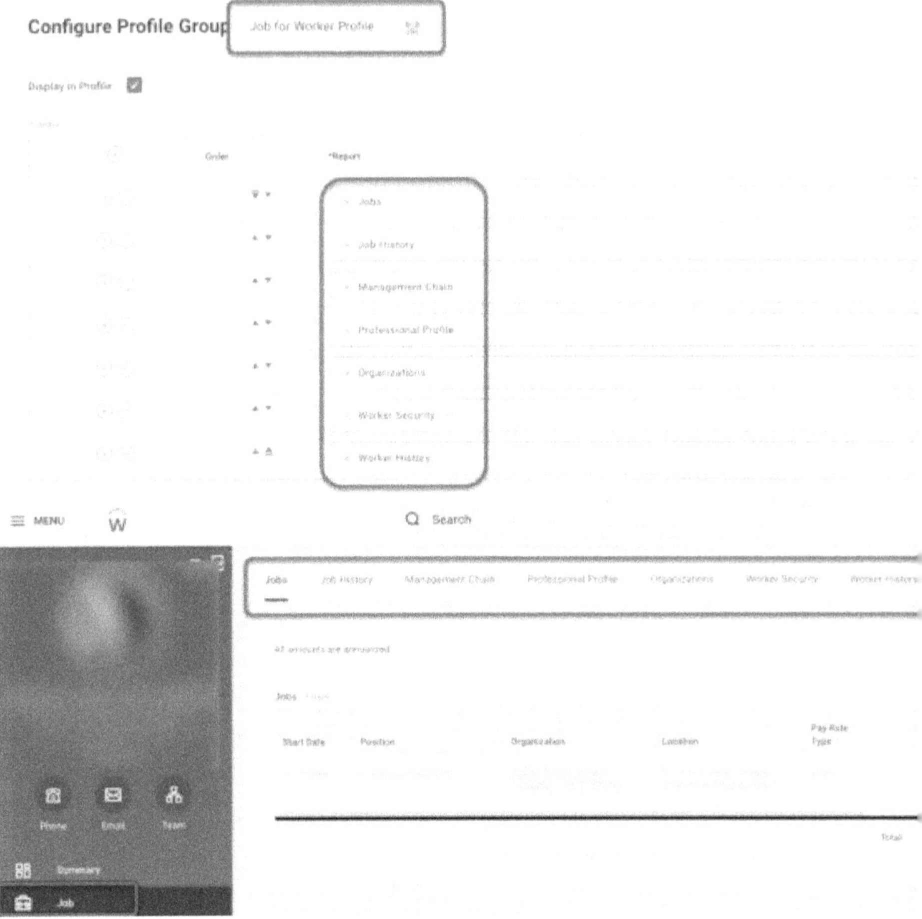

December 2022

Many profile 'sections' in Workday have the option to choose which 'tabs' you want to display and in what order.

Use the 'Configure Profile Group' task to make changes:

- Select to section of the profile you want to edit from the drop-down. There are hundreds to choose from (depending on what modules you have).

- Update the tabs that you want to turn on or off, or reorder.

- A common one to add is the 'Additional Data' tab, which shows your custom objects for that particular profile/data object.

- You can also add reports as new tabs.

Adjust Profile pages to match your users' needs! (Part 4 of 4)

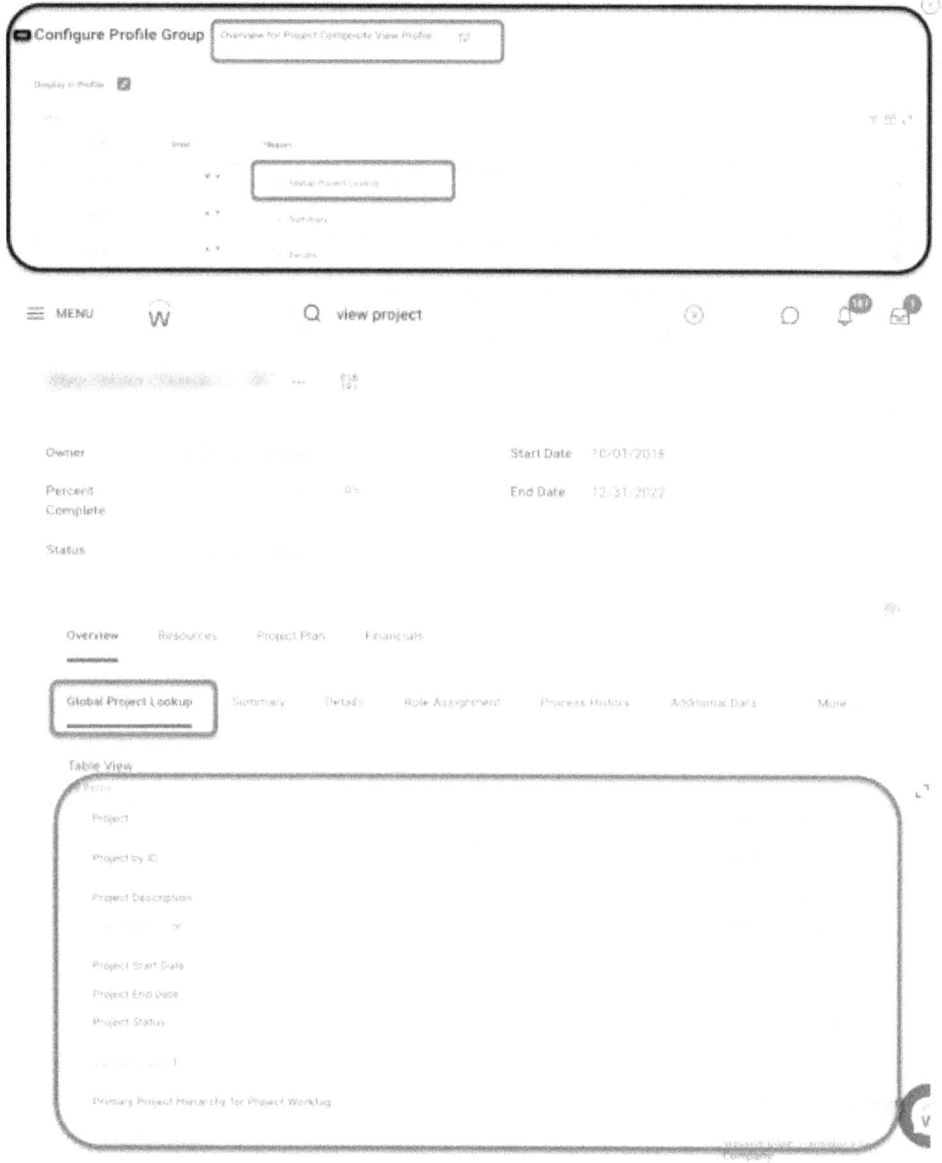

December 2022

Add custom reports as Tabs on your profile pages. You can do this with the 'Configure Profile Group' task.

As an example, one company that I worked with used the Workday Project module. The users didn't like the summary page that Workday provides as the default. So, I created a 'Transposed' report (which is like an Excel Pivot table view of the data) which only showed one project at a time and the exact fields the users wanted to see.

As you can see in the screenshot, I set the profile up so that it would be the first tab that showed up when users opened the Workday Project profile page.

Another example that I have highlighted in a previous post is to add the 'Worker Security' Report to the Worker profile page in the Job section. This report shows all the security groups that the user is a part of. If you haven't seen that before, check it out in a GMS tenant, if you have access to one. You can easily recreate it in your tenant.

Note- Not all reports can be added to Profile Groups. They have to be created on the correct business object for that Profile and have a filter that meets to prompt requirements of the profile group. Sometimes I have had to experiment to find the right combination.

For direct links to each LinkedIn post, please visit
KeithBitikofer.com/Workday-Gold-SF-Links/

Leveraging Custom Objects

Custom Objects Overview

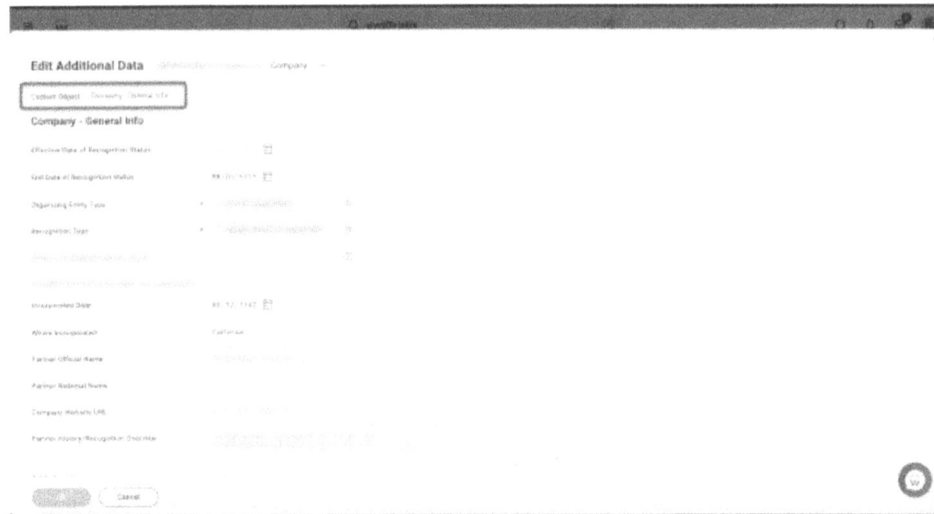

May 2022

There will always be data that you want to store in Workday that Workday doesn't have a standard field for. So, what do you do?

Consider using Custom Fields, which sit in Custom Objects.

You can add custom objects to 30 or so standard Workday objects (such as Worker, Supplier, Position, Customer, and Project objects).

Be aware that you are limited to 100 or 200 custom fields per standard Workday object, depending on what modules are part of your subscription. So-be strategic about what custom fields you create or you will run out!

1- Make sure that there isn't another way to put this data in standard Workday (or even something like a 'custom ID' on Workers).

2- Determine who needs to edit or view this data. You need to add a security domain to the new custom object that you are going to create.

3- Consider who will be updating this data. In my experience, this only works for heavy users of Workday that will be willing to continually update these fields. The fields show on the 'additional data' tab of the Objects and users that don't often use Workday will never find them to update them. (Create an Extend app for those situations).

Remember: The only thing worse than NOT having this data in your system is to actually have it in your system and have it be OUT of DATE due to no one UPDATING it. Then people assume it is accurate when it is NOT!

Recommendation: Leverage the delivered functionality as much as possible, or think twice if you really need a custom object. As long as you take the limitations into consideration as you design your solution, they can still be very helpful.

Also strongly consider using a Workday Extend to build custom apps instead of Custom Objects, if you have that option.

Leveraging Custom Objects (Example 1)

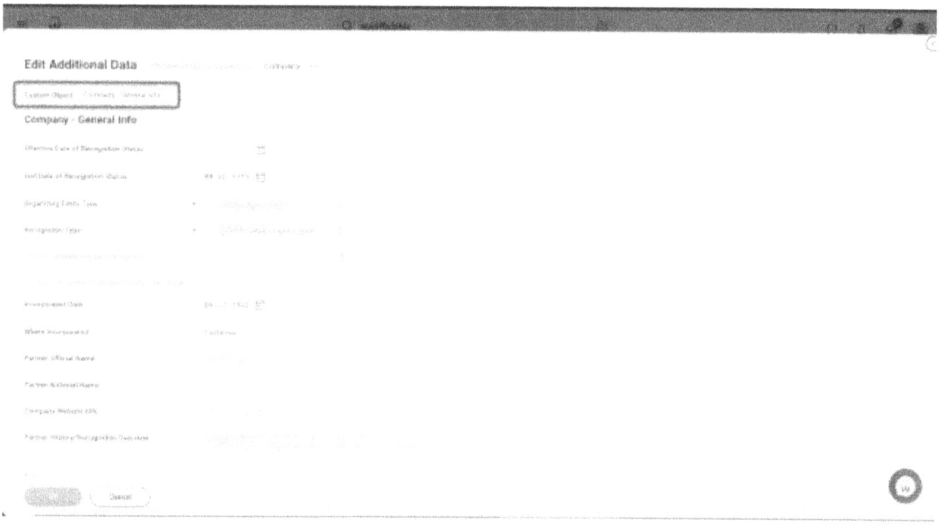

June 2022

I have created custom objects for lots of different scenarios. Sometimes it is for something basic like an extra value that we need to know about every company set up in our system. Other times, it is a whole set of data that actually replaces an old system.

Initial example: A common use case is that you just need a field to store a value on a standard Workday object. See the screenshot. For example, on Companies, maybe you have multiple companies in your tenant and you need to track where they were incorporated or the year they were incorporated. Or, on the Project object, maybe this project is also tracked in Jira and you need the Jira project ID in Workday for integrations.

Create an object called: 'General Info'.

For consistency's sake (across different objects), I always create an object called 'General Info' for these types of scenarios. Then I set the security up so that everyone with access to that company, project, etc. can SEE the data, but only a limited group can actually UPDATE the data.

This could be on the Worker, Project, Supplier, Customer, Company, etc. standard objects for individual fields that we want to track that Workday doesn't have a standard field for.

Multi Company Contact list (Example 2)

June 2022

If you have multiple companies in the same Workday tenant, you don't necessarily want everyone in one company to see all the people in the other companies in your tenant, even for basic contact info. But it can be really helpful to know who is the primary contact for HR, Finance, etc. in the other companies.

So, you can a 'Company - Contact Info' custom object on the company object. Then each company can maintain a list of who the primary contacts are at their company and how they prefer to be contacted. Sometimes this is also helpful because the 'role' someone plays in a company may not always match the 'position' they are in. So, this allows much more flexibility.

We created a custom list of the types of roles that we would like to have for each company. Then we give an admin user in each company the ability to update this list as they need to. We have various reports that any staff can run to access this basis contact list.

We also have an integration that uses this list to generate a PDF (BIRT report) of all the crisis management contacts. It emails it to anyone listed as a crisis management contact on a monthly basis. That way they can have the PDF on their phones and don't even have to log into Workday in the midst of a crisis.

Tracking interactions / CRM lite (Example 3)

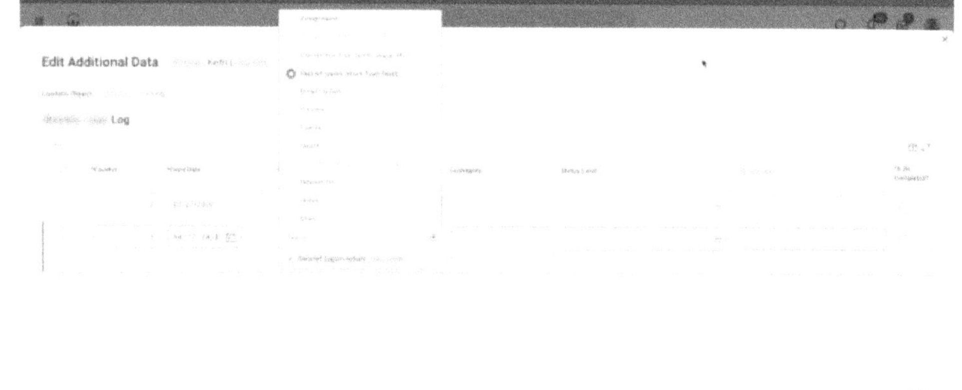

June 2022

Suppose that you have scenarios where a designated HR person is responsible for checking in with certain workers and you want to be able to track these interactions. You could use a CRM system to do that, or you could create a 'multi-instance' custom object on the Worker object. The multi-instance functionality allows you to have multiple rows of data for the various fields. See the attached screenshot.

In this case, there is the drop-down shown as what we call the 'event type'. As in, what type of event is the HR person recording?

Typically I would make the date field the primary key field. But in this case, they could have multiple rows or 'events' on the same day. So we added a 'counter' column that the user just adds the next number in sequence for each new row.

We then created ESI (extract single instance) calc fields to grab the most recent row, or the most recent row with a specific event type for various reports. For example, we wanted to track event types to ensure that these HR staff were consistently connecting with their assigned staff (maybe 4x a year).

You could also do this on the supplier, project, or customer objects and you could use Extend to create a fancier version of this. There is a Community post about a Workday customer who created an Extend app and doing this to track interactions with their customers about payments. You can find this link via the link at the end of this chapter.

For direct links to each LinkedIn post, please visit
KeithBitikofer.com/Workday-Gold-SF-Links/

Leverage Workday Dashboards

Leverage Workday dashboards, Supplier Accounts

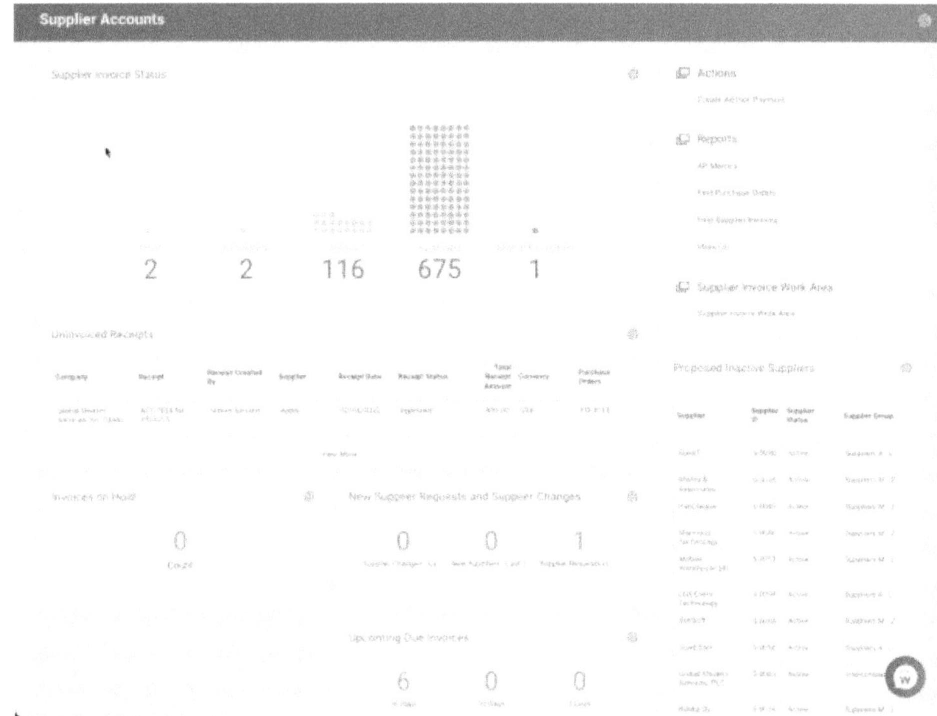

February 2022

Another useful dashboard is the: 'Supplier Accounts for Supplier Accounts'. It is very helpful for Finance / AP. As usual, I'd suggest that you include links to the tasks and reports your team regularly uses on the 'menu' section of the dashboard.

Supplier Performance Dashboard Community page. You can find this link via the link at the end of this chapter.

You may also be interested in the 'Accounts Payables Dashboard' Community page. You can find this link via the link at the end of this chapter.

Workday continues to add more great dashboards like these (including the 'System Health Dashboard'), but I wanted to highlight some key ones this week!

(note- the screenshot isn't blurred because it came from a Workday GMS demo tenant).

Workday Dashboards: Payroll

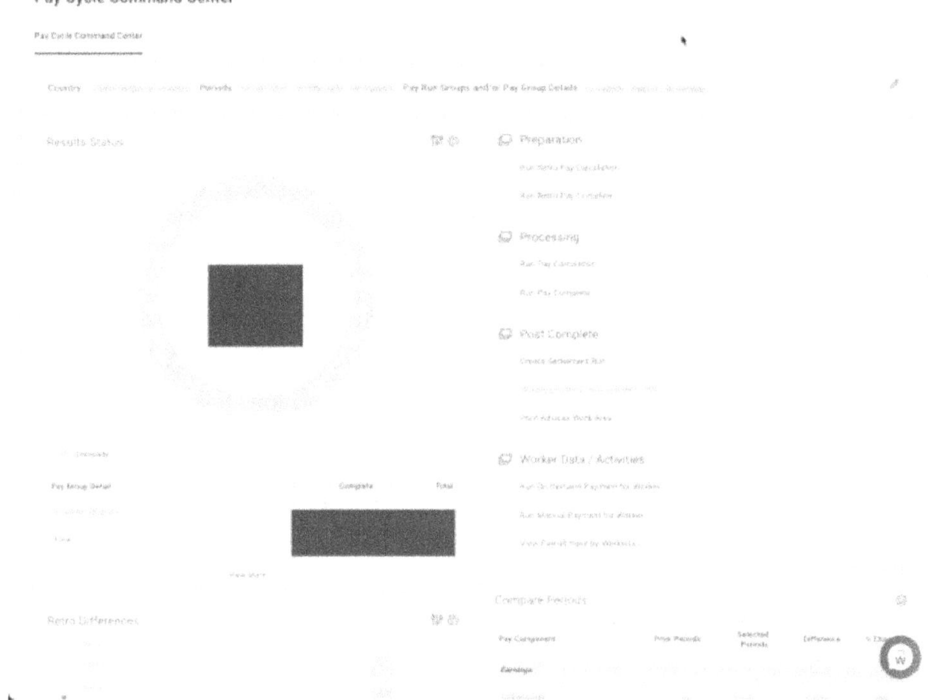

February 2022

Leverage Workday Provided Dashboards:

Workday has several preconfigured dashboards related to Payroll:

Pay Cycle Command Center

Payroll Compliance Updates

Payroll Year End

These have been a huge value add for payroll teams. When the Pay Cycle Command Center came out, one payroll user I showed it to was very excited because of all the manual effort (in Excel) it was going to save her!

On the Pay Cycle Command Center dashboard, I also added their commonly used tasks as menu items (on the right side), in the order that they do them, to streamline their processes.

Workday Documentation in Community:

Setup Considerations for Payroll Dashboards

Payroll Year-End Dashboard

(You can find these links via the link at the end of this chapter.)

Definitely check these out if you aren't already using them!

The "System Health Dashboard" is also pretty decent. It started out a bit so-so but I've gotten some useful metrics recently as I was troubleshooting.

Team Performance is another.

Workday Dashboards: Report Administrator

January 2022

For Workday Customers - If you are responsible for creating and monitoring reports in your tenant, you should really set up the 'Report Administrator for Report Administrator' Custom Dashboard. See the link below for instructions on how to set it up in your tenant. To my knowledge, this is often not set up by implementation consultants during your initial project.

Workday has provided a series of reports that you can add to the dashboard including:

- Custom Reports Exception by Owner
- Custom Reports Not Run
- Recently Created and Modified Reports
- Recently Updated Calc Fields
- Scheduled Reports that will fail
- Slowest Reports Run in Background

Each of these reports highlights a key area that someone should be monitoring in your tenant.

For example, if you have many people creating reports in your tenant, the number of custom reports that haven't been run recently can grow quickly. This then creates additional maintenance when Workday creates new versions of fields (and you have to update your reports to use the new versions, etc.). So, I'd recommend using the 'Custom Reports Not Run' to review and potentially delete reports that haven't been used in the last 12- 18 months. Just make sure you don't delete any reports that are only used during the year-end or annual review processes.

It is also helpful to add links to report maintenance tasks that you don't use often, such as 'Delete Temporary Report Definitions' or 'Transfer Ownership of Custom Reports'.

Documentation in Workday Community:

Concept Report Administrator Dashboard (You can find this link via the link at the end of this chapter.)

Create Custom Workday Dashboards

November 2021

Ideas for improving end-user engagement with Workday: Use Dashboards-give users more reasons to use Workday!

Create multi-tab Dashboards with:

- Charts and graphs of useful summary HR or Finance data, with links to related tasks or documentation

- Charts and graphs of useful data from other systems by using Prism to store/pull data.

- Create a 'one-stop shop' view around a topic per tab: include documents in Workday, links to Workday tasks, use the bulletin functionality to organize lists of links to internal or external videos, links to Google drives or Google Docs, etc.

For direct links to each LinkedIn post, please visit
KeithBitikofer.com/Workday-Gold-SF-Links/

HCM-Specific Functionality Highlights

Leverage Org Studio

May 2022

Org Studio is a drag-and-drop tool that facilitates planning for and implementing organizational / staffing restructures in your company.

Maybe your leadership is considering moving a team or department from one director to another. What might that look like?

With Org Studio, you can create several potential new staffing structure scenarios, share them with leadership to review, and then click to implement them. We have found it really helpful!

Since this is not needed during an initial Workday implementation (because you are mass-loading your staffing structures), I suspect that many companies aren't even aware this functionality exists. It's very cool! (Ok. I'm a geek!)

To check these out, visit the link at the end of this chapter:

Watch this overview video or just look at the slides.

Documentation on setting up Org Studio

Leverage the 'Union Membership' functionality for tracking Memberships and more

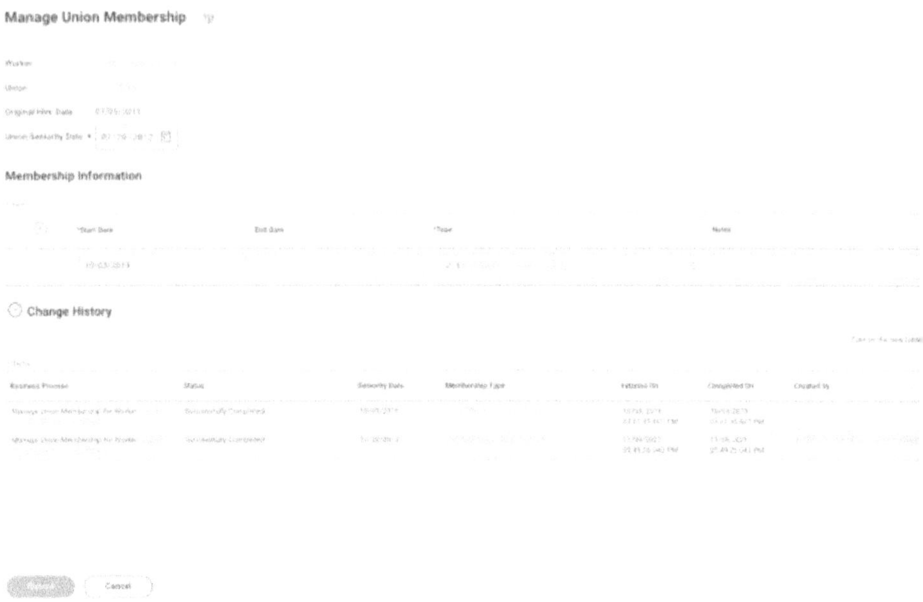

April 2022

Now, before you say that we don't have a union, so this doesn't apply to me, hang in with me for a moment.

Do you need to keep track of your staff being part of any kind of memberships? Just think of it as another 'container' to which you can add staff. Maybe you have some types of clubs at your company, and you want to know when they joined it, how long they were in it, and what level of 'membership' they had. Maybe there is staff that needs to have access to some level of the HR data for the staff in these 'memberships'.

All this can be done with the Union Membership functionality! And, you can CHANGE the NAME of 'Union Membership' to be whatever you want it to be! (In the 'HR Compliance' section of the Maintain Custom Labels task)

There BPs related to it, so you can include approvals or 'to do' steps (Union Membership Event). You will have the transaction history of when people were added when they left, and who did the transactions. You can define the 'membership types' and the 'membership groups (called 'unions' by default).

You can also use segmented security to allow certain people to see the contact info about everyone in a specific group/union. I work with one company that uses it heavily for tracking memberships and membership levels.

Leverage Worker Documents / Document Categories

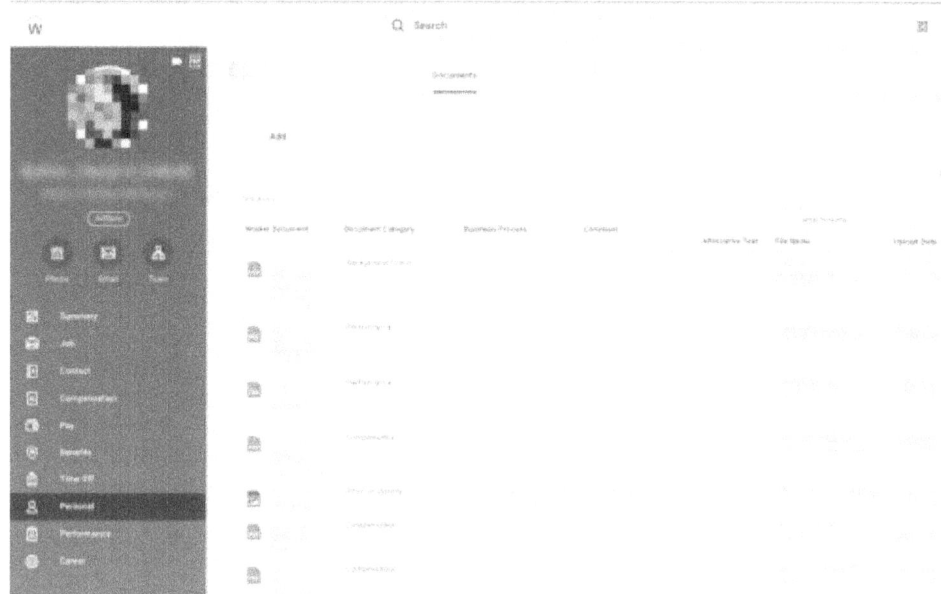

February 2022

Where does your organization store Worker-related documents?

When we first went live with Workday many years ago, we had paper files (and a scanning project going on), files on SharePoint, files on shared server drives, and probably some on local computers.

Then, at Workday Rising, some of us saw a session where a Workday customer talked about how they had mass-loaded over a million worker documents into Workday. That inspired us.

The next year, we moved over 100k worker-related documents into Workday! From that point forward, we have leveraged Workday Documents, and Document Categories (similar to directories on a server) combined with Segmented Security. This way users can only see the document categories, and the documents in them, that they have security and a business reason to have access to.

To be clear Workday is NOT a document management system. But it does quite well at storing and securing HR documents that our HR staff need to store and access.

One tool that has been especially helpful is a .net app (credit to Mike Mohr at McKee Foods!). It allows you to mass load all the documents in a directory, with the file names starting with the worker ID, into a specific Document Category. I'm sure you could do something similar with a Studio integration, but this tool has been hugely helpful!

Link to more information about this tool on Workday Community

Note- we also use all the standard functionality for collecting documents during the Workday Recruiting application process, document delivery task, etc. But there are always other worker files that need to be stored in a central location as well.

Leverage Mentorship functionality

We all need a coach or Mentor at various times of our lives, such as when we go through transitions. Maybe when you first start working at a company, or are a manager for the first time, etc. We want our staff to grow and to set them up for success. But how do we be intentional about that?

Workday has Mentorship functionality as part of the HCM core module. There are standard tasks/reports for Find a Mentor, My Mentorships, My Teams Mentorships, View Mentorships, etc.

I have seen people include this as a step in onboarding or in a Workday Journey for onboarding, or you could manually set them up at certain points in your processes.

You can set up different mentorship types to segment out the types of mentorship that your company offers. Maybe you assign a specific HR person to follow up with new people during their first 90 days at your company, but you also have a team member assigned to be an 'orientation mentor' for new staff. So, you could create two different types of mentorship for these different scenarios.

You can track your team's capacity for mentorships using the My Team's Mentorship report. Maybe you don't want the HR person to have more than 10 people to mentor at a given point in time.

I have created reports that listed new staff and which existing staff were responsible for 'helping' them in different ways. They were set up as a Workday Mentor for the new staff, but on the reports, we used our internal names such as 'HR Guide' as the column heading.

One note to be aware of: This may have changed, but when either the mentor OR a mentee got terminated then the mentorship relationship will still be in open state and will need to be manually closed.

Leverage International Assignment Functionality

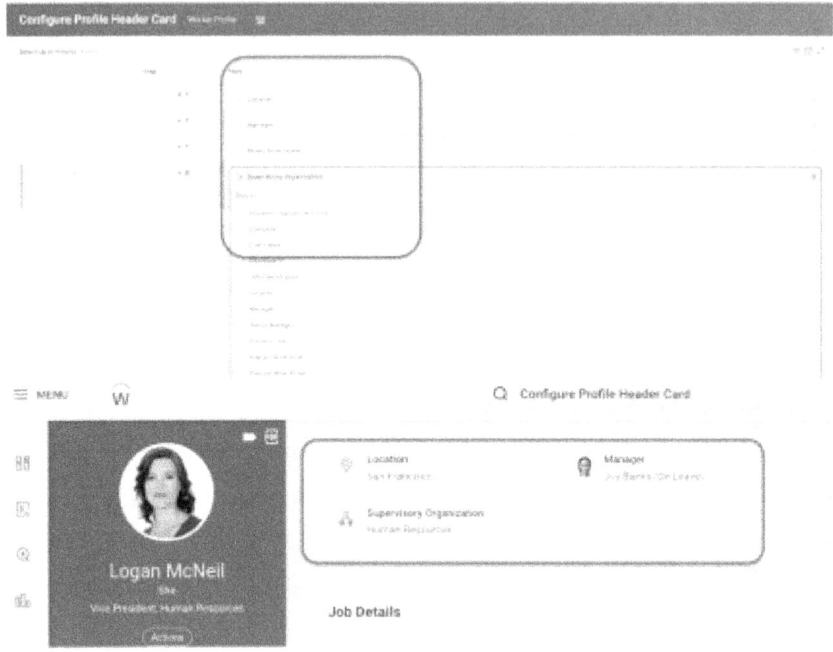

January 2023

The International Assignment (IA) allows you to have a staff person with a 'home position' in their primary company and then have an additional position in another company in your tenant.

Maybe they have a USA-based position as their primary position, but for 6 months they are going to be temporarily working for your London-based division (which may be a separate company in your tenant). You could use the IA functionality for that.

A couple of other quick notes:

- It can have its own onboarding process (this helps if you have a checklist of items staff have to go through before starting their new/additional assignment).

- It also works with Workday Payroll and you can change the name/label of it to something that uses the terminology your company uses for this type of position.

- It is also now incorporated into the updated 'Add Additional Job' functionality instead of just a standalone task.

For more information, check out the documentation International and Domestic Assignments on Workday community. You can find this link at the end of this chapter.

Leverage Safety Incident Tracking functionality

November 2022

It is part of the Workday core HCM, so any HCM customer can leverage it.

There is a task called 'Report Safety Incident'.

There is a summary dashboard called the 'Safety Incident Dashboard' (pictured).

Part of the reason that this functionality is interesting to me is that you can set up your own incident types ('maintain incident types') and a list of other values for the drop-downs. While you may not have enough work-related injuries to justify setting this up in Workday, do you have other 'incidents' or investigations that you need to track?

The Safety Incident functionality allows you to set up questionnaires for those involved in an incident for investigations, to collect whatever information you need to collect, defined by you.

If you have access to a GMS tenant, check it out there. It is turned on in the demo tenants.

You can find the link via the link to documentation on Workday Community via the link at the end of this chapter.

Leverage Workday Committees

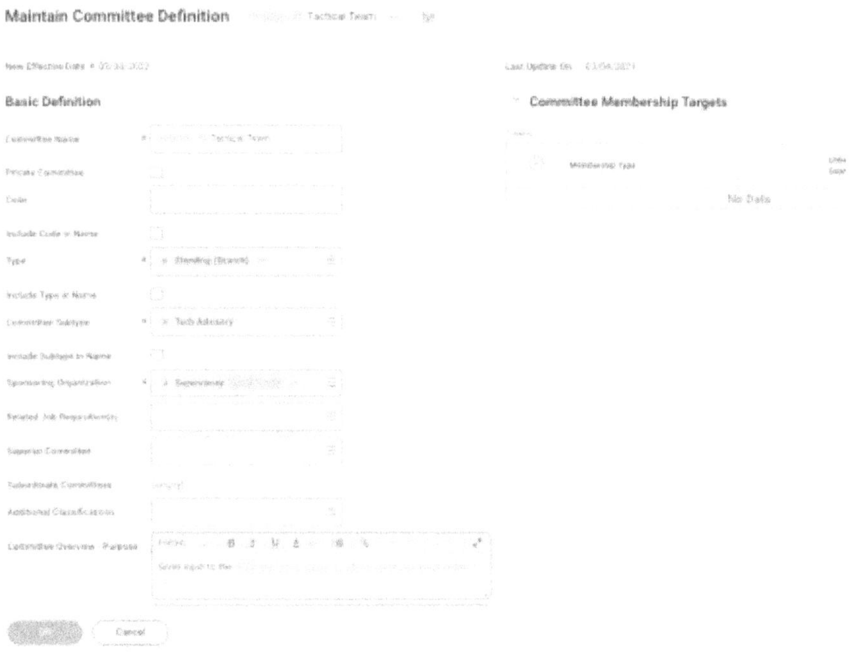

March 2023

Workday Committees was originally created for the Higher Education space, but it is part of the core HCM Workday functionality. It is available to all companies. You just have to turn it on and decide how you want to use it.

Admittedly the terminology used for field names are Higher Ed focused, but it will still make sense to non Higher Ed users as well.

A common use that I have seen for this is for tracking people on company boards. Some people add all their board members in their tenant as employees or contingent workers. But committees are another option to track all the contact info of your board members, without taking up 'seats' for your Workday subscription FSE counts.

Examples of Committee functionality:

- You can have different 'types' of committees

- Can track events and meeting notes

- A key thing is that they can include people with their contact info and photos from outside of your company

- Committees are effectively dated. So you can change to committees over time (who was on the committee 2 years ago?)

- Membership types (membership in the committee)

- Membership start date and term end date

- Includes some BPs

There are reports to list all your committees and to list everyone in a specific committee with all their contact info.

For direct links to each LinkedIn post, please visit
KeithBitikofer.com/Workday-Gold-SF-Links/

Cross-Platform Workday Tips

Leverage Quicklinks!

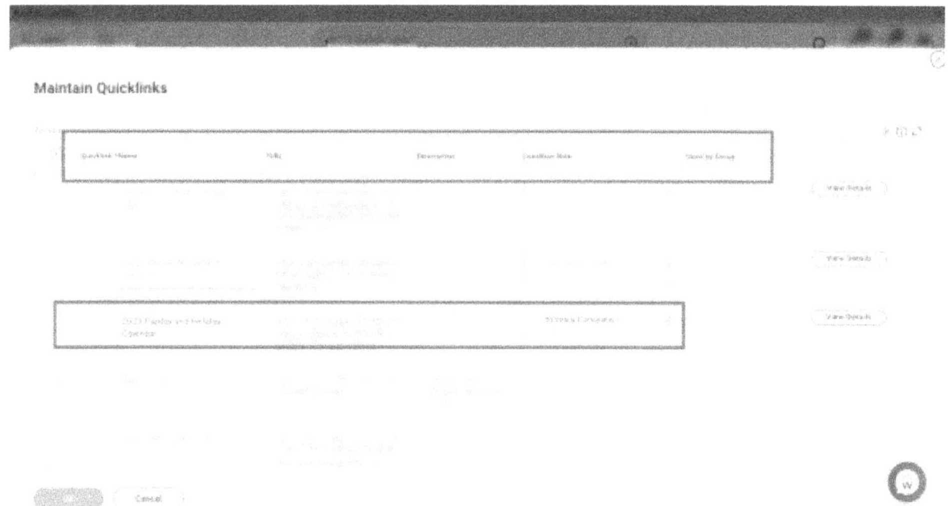

December 2021

Workday Quicklinks are simply URL links. You can add links to go to a Workday Help Article in Workday, to other things in Workday, to Google Docs (maybe with some of your HR or Expenses policies), to your healthcare vendor's websites, or to YouTube videos.

You can use Workday Quicklinks on Dashboards to link out to external websites such as:

- your benefits provider's website
- a Google doc with your company HR Policies
- to other key systems at your company
- a YouTube video for new managers

This way you can help your users get easy access to resources that you know they need!

Use 'Maintain Quicklinks' to create them.

You can add them to dashboards using 'Maintain Dashboards'. Within the setup for a given tab of the dashboard, select the Quicklink as an 'External Link' under the 'Menu' section.

You can also create a quicklink group to group specific URLs together, for use with a custom report filtered for that quicklink group.

Leverage Workday Languages!

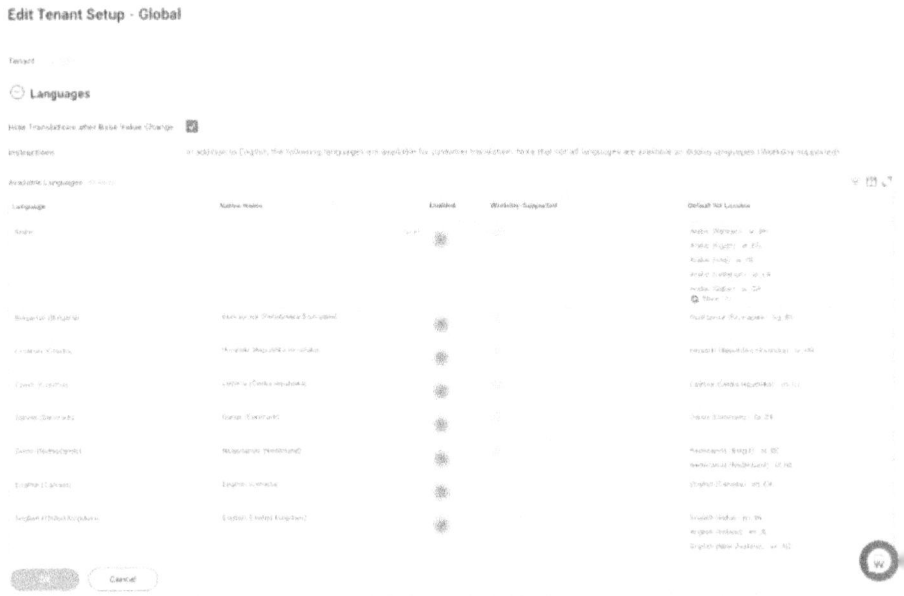

May 2022

Did you know that Workday has the menus and key parts of the system translated into 43 languages?

Which do you have turned on? Go the 'Edit Tenant Setup - Global' to see.

I think that most Workday customers have at least some workers who aren't native English speakers. So, even if all your data (job descriptions, etc.) are in English, for someone who isn't completely comfortable with English, having all the menus shown in a language they are more comfortable with can be really helpful!

Customers used to have a pay extra to leverage the additional languages. This is now part of the regular subscription costs.

Leverage Custom labels

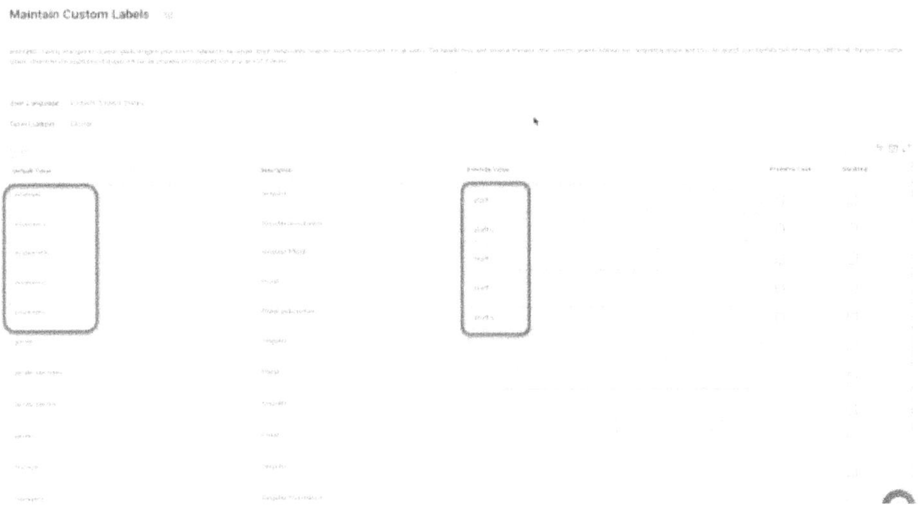

November 2022

There is Workday 'lingo' that users need to learn to fully leverage Workday. Fortunately, Workday does give the option to tailor some of the Workday terms to be terms that make more sense for your company or organization's context.

For example, maybe you are a nonprofit or association that has several staff types, such as paid staff, interns, and volunteers. So, the default term of 'employee' for everyone in your organization doesn't work well. Volunteers don't think of themselves as 'employees' because they don't get paid for their effort, but they do want to be seen as part of the organization, so the term 'staff' may work better than 'employee'.

Workday gives you the opportunity to change the 'labels' in your Workday tenant at a global level. So, for the scenario above, you can change the label 'employee' to 'staff', as shown in the screenshot. I've also heard that some retail companies change 'employee' to 'associate'.

Use the 'Maintain Custom Labels' task to see all the different labels that can be updated. There are 22 Label Categories and over 350 field labels that you can edit (some are different versions of the same term such as, singular, possessive, plural, of a given label).

Other examples include changing the 'Additional Job Description' to 'Internal Job Description'

Leverage Hierarchies

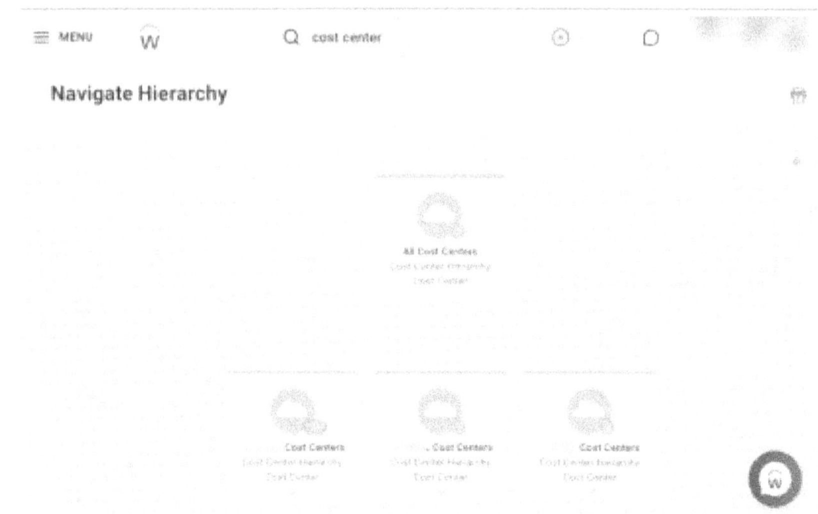

January 2023

Hierarchies are a way to 'group' different types of data in Workday. You can use hierarchies for filtering reports as well as security so that certain groups of users can only see certain hierarchies.

For example, you can create hierarchies with the following data sets:

- Companies

- Customers

- Cost Centers

- Projects

- Custom Organizations

- Locations (for example, this can be broad for something like continents and as granular as an office floor)

Then you can use the 'Navigate Hierarchy' to navigate up and down the levels in a viewer similar to the Organizational Chart viewer.

We have used it in all the above scenarios, both for reporting purposes and security.

Leverage Workday Bulletin functionality

April 2023

The Workday Bulletin functionality allows you to create additional 'boxes' on Dashboards. See picture. You can add links (Quicklinks or videos) with a small graphic and summary text to each row in the Bulletin sections.

For example, you can create links and bookmarks to policy documents in Google Docs (or other document tools) and add them to a Bulletin. The advantage of this is that you can secure the Google document so that only a few people can edit it. Then have the links and summary text set up in a Workday Bulletin / Dashboard. This way the authorized users can update the Google documents as often as necessary, without having to update the Bulletin / Dashboard in Workday, (which takes a fairly high level of security to do).

Use the 'Create Bulletin Worklet' task to build the Bulletins.

You can also add condition rules so that they dynamically appear/hide on a dashboard based on attributes of the current user or event. This can be helpful if you only want to have it show on the dashboard until certain tasks are completed, etc.

Customize the settings on your Workday Home Cards

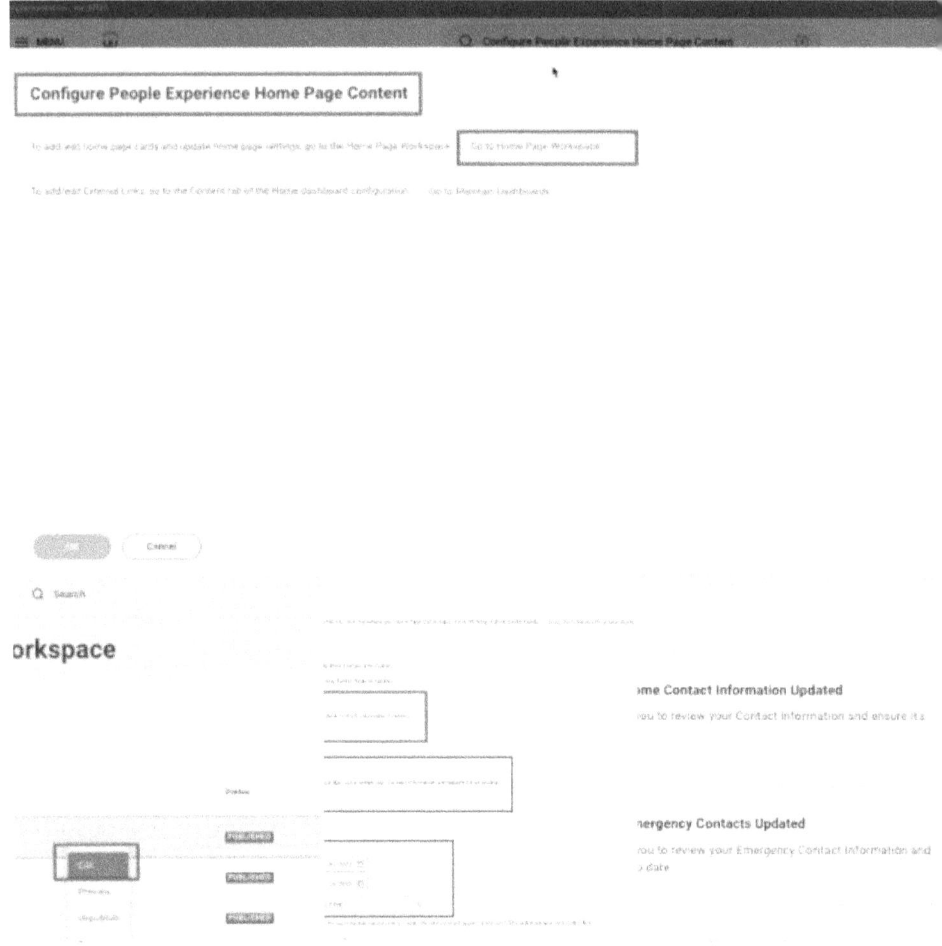

March 2023

Workday has various 'cards' that you can turn on that will then be displayed in the center of the Workday Home screen.

Several helpful cards include Payslips, Change 1095-C Printing Election, Birthday for Workers, etc.

You can configure aspects of some of these cards. For certain cards, you can now change the title, sub-title, and create a custom schedule about when that card shows up. This is really helpful for some of the cards like 'Change My Work Contact Information' or 'Change My Emergency Contacts' cards.

By default, these cards show up and just stay there. So, a worker could see the card, and click on it to edit their information, but then the card still stays there, even after the worker did what you wanted them to do.

Now, with the ability to create a custom schedule for the card, you can set it up to show up every January for a month, or whatever works best for your staff.

To Edit the configuration, go to: Configure People Experience Home Page Content

Select 'Home Cards Workspace'

Select 'Edit' on the card you want to configure (if that card is configurable).

For direct links to each LinkedIn post, please visit
KeithBitikofer.com/Workday-Gold-SF-Links/

Other

Leverage Workday Worksheets

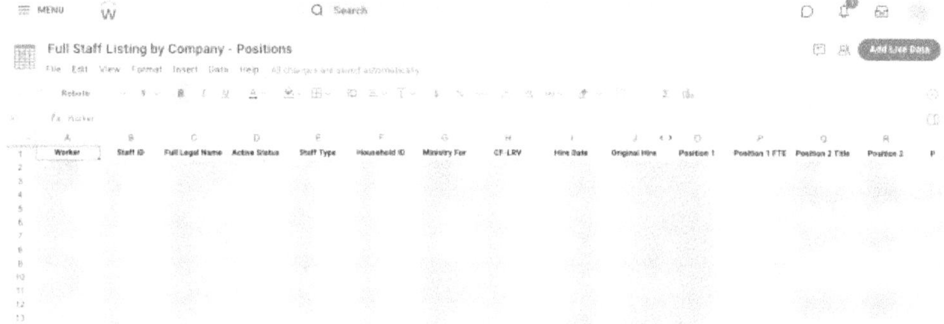

November 2022

Workday Worksheets is a tool that is spreadsheet-like but within Workday. You can share them like a Google Sheet and you can send report data into a Worksheet. Then you can add to the data (columns, formulas, etc.) and click a button to pull or 'refresh' the data from Workday.

It is also part of the Workday Slide functionality. The 'Slides' (like a PowerPoint slide) can pull data from a Worksheet to quickly update Workday Slides. For example, you could have a Workday Slide presentation with various headcount numbers or financial numbers, being pulled from a Worksheet. Once you have this Slide presentation built, each month or quarter, you can quickly update the Worksheet (click the 'updated' button to re-pull the numbers from the reports) and then do the same thing for the Slide presentation. It can be a huge time saver!

You can find more resources on Workday Community via the link at the end of this chapter for the following:

Introduction to Worksheets

Setup Worksheets

Workday Slides

Summary of New Changes for Worksheets

What are Workday Discovery boards?

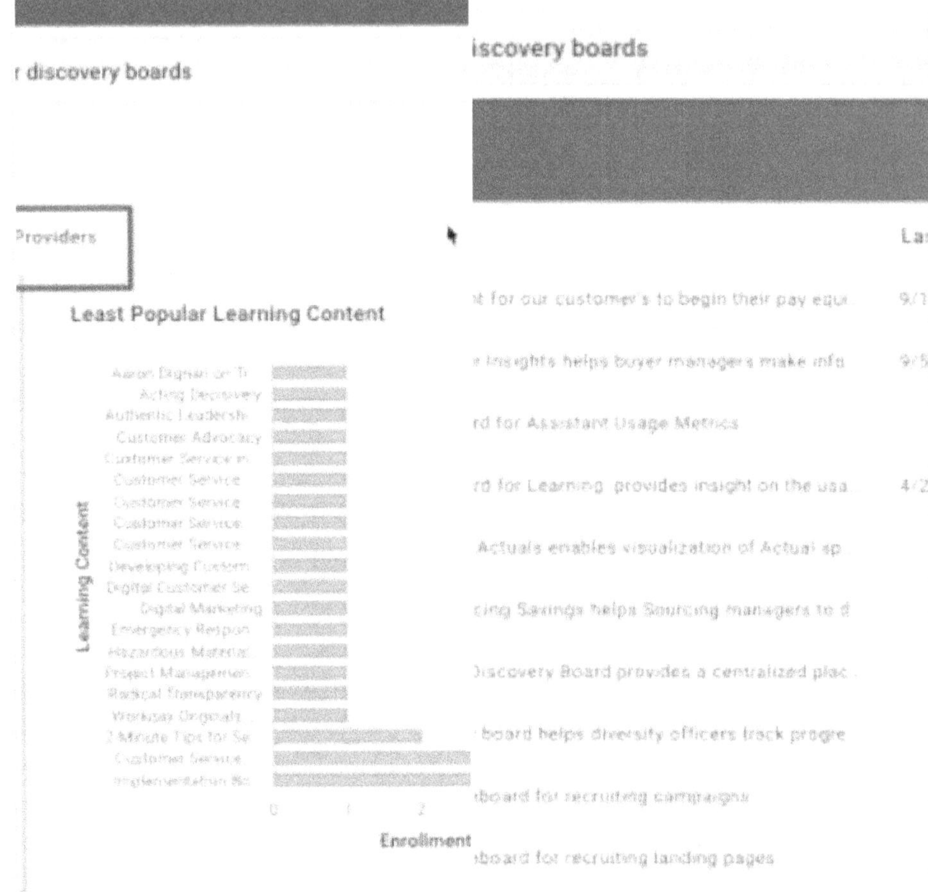

November 2022

Workday Discovery boards are another way to create reports in Workday. It uses a 'drag and drop' process to create new reports.

You can create a dashboard with multiple tabs and multiple visualizations on each tab. You can add at least 10 or more visualizations to a tab (vs the 6 you can add to a typical Workday dashboard). While it started with just charts, you can now also create visualizations that are rows and columns, like an advanced report. There isn't a way yet to create ones that are like a composite report (for year-over-year comparisons, etc.).

Workday has recently released a set of examples or 'Delivered Discovery Boards' which you can enable in your tenants to help you get started. (You have to enable the 'Discovery Boards: Managed Delivered Discovery Boards' domain.) If you have access to a GMS tenant, search on 'Delivered Discovery Boards' to see the list. Then you select one to view, copy it, and click the link to go to Drive to select and view it.

Check out the 'Discovery Boards' summary page in Community. You can find this link via the link at the end of this chapter. It is a great list of resources to help you learn more about Discovery boards, videos, examples, instructions on how to enable it, etc.

They have recently added new report types, such as Waterfall, Heatmap, Scatterplot, and KPI, some of which aren't even available in Matrix reports.

You can also convert visualization into a matrix report.

What are your favorite uses of Workday Prism (data warehouse module)?

July 2023

- Bringing in historical HR position or Finance data from a legacy system and merging it with Workday core data

- Bringing in data from external systems to combine, transform, and then display in Workday or merge with Workday data

- Summarizing Workday Core HR or Finance data and sharing it with staff that don't have security access to the transactional data

- Using it with Workday's Accounting Center to pull and summarize financial transaction data from other company systems

Then you can use the standard Workday reporting tools (Advanced, Matrix, and composite reports or discovery boards) to create reports and dashboards.

Workday Prism has been a great tool for many Workday customers that I talk to or work with.

Use the 'Where Used' tab EVERY time you change Calc Fields and the 'Used' tab on Condition rules!

September 2022

We once had a benefits issue with an eligibility rule. The benefits consultant found the issue and fixed it. They successfully tested that scenario and then moved it to Prod. The next day nobody could clock in for time tracking and several other things were broken.

It turned out that this condition rule was used in 14 different places! We quickly changed things back and everything worked again. Then we created a new condition rule for the Benefits BPs to use.

Always look at the 'where used' and 'usage' tabs- even when you are in a hurry to 'fix' something!

Leverage Workday Help (part 1 of 2)

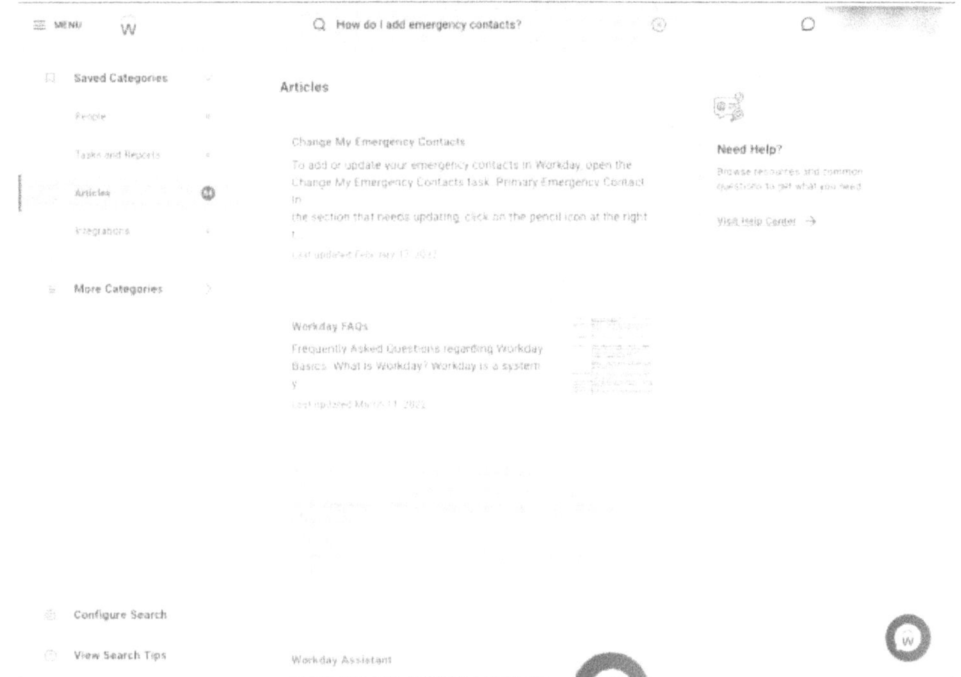

March 2022

Workday 'Help' is a relatively new module that is available as an additional SKU for purchase. The Help functionality includes two components:

- Articles (knowledge base articles)

- Case Management

I have posted about this in the past. But I'm still surprised about how many people that I talk to that don't know about it. I think this is a module that EVERY Workday customer should seriously consider (even if you only use Workday HCM or Workday Financials).

I'd also like to encourage all Workday Sales Reps to consider including this on ANY new customer contract that you are working on. I'm glad to talk with you about this as well! :-)

Let's focus on the 'Articles' part for this post.

Over the years, the customer that I worked at made lots of job aids to help our users find what they were looking for in Workday, and understand Workday Terminology (i.e. What is an 'International Assignment'?). We used to load these job aid documents (as PDFs) as system documents and added them to dashboards such as one we called "Workday Helps and Resources".

Many other customers put their job aids in SharePoint or a variety of other intranet-type solutions. But then you are forcing people to LEAVE Workday to learn about how to USE Workday. My goal is always to keep our users in Workday for as much as reasonably possible.

Now that we can create Articles, the customer that I worked with converted all of our job aids to Articles. In the past, people had to know to go to our custom Dashboard to try and find the job aid they were looking for. Now they can do a Workday search, such as 'How do I add emergency contacts?' and it will bring up a list of Articles (see screenshot).

AI has been talked about a lot this year. Workday has been analyzing all the Articles with their machine learning tools for several years. The machine learning tools with Workday Help analyze the article content and then use the results to improve the search process. With Workday Help, we can do full-sentence searches within Workday- at least for Articles.

We have also created Articles with the definitions for specific Workday or Company-specific terms that are confusing to users - such as "What does 'International Assignment' mean in our context?".

You can create a link directly to an Article, which you can then add to a 'menu' or 'bulletin' on a custom dashboard. We do this to provide easy access to help Articles specifically about that Dashboard or Extend Apps that we make available via a Dashboard.

Articles allow you to keep your users in the Workday tenant and you can include links to business processes, reports, and other Articles within the article text.

If you are using the Workday Assistant chatbot, the Articles show up there as well. This can be a huge help for new staff or users who aren't heavy users of Workday.

Leverage Workday Help (part 2 of 2)

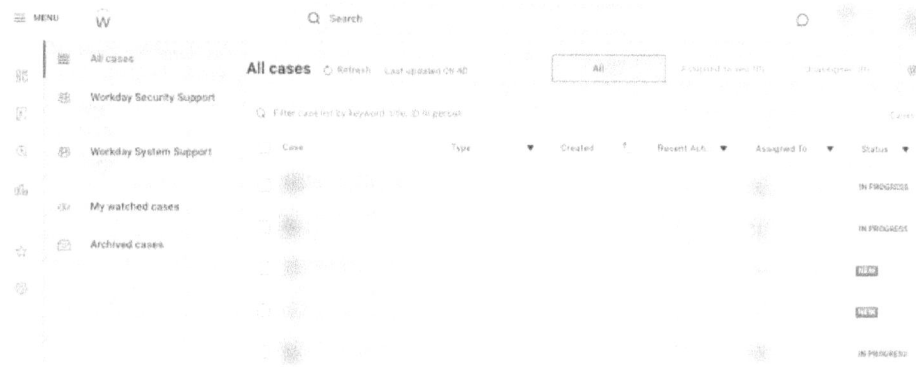

March 2022

Workday 'Help' is a relatively new module that is available as an additional SKU for purchase. The Help functionality includes two components:

- Case Management
- Articles (knowledge base articles)

I have posted about this in the past. But I'm still surprised about how many people that I talk to that don't know about it. I think this is a module that EVERY Workday customer should seriously consider (even if you only use Workday HCM or Workday Financials).

Let's focus on Case Management for this post.

There are lots of ticketing systems out there. Why have a ticketing type system in Workday?

Many years ago, at one of the first Workday Extend Hackathons, I was part of a team that had the idea to build a ticketing system in Workday. Our thought was that usually tickets/requests that someone wants to create inherently need to know information that is already in Workday. For example, you have a payroll question- Workday already knows who your company's payroll staff are. You may need to request an upgrade to your laptop- Workday knows who your manager is (that should approve this request), Workday knows the IT staff (to order the parts), etc.

Workday Help / Case Management is built on those ideas, plus many others.

Workday Help is advertised as being for HR-type cases/ tickets. But, from my standpoint, it is a ticketing system, which could be used for any type of ticket. (You can even change the name/label of it). Its functionality is tightly tied to the existing questionnaire functionality and the knowledge-based articles that come with the Workday Help module.

When you create the various case types that your company needs, you have the option to say that certain case types are 'confidential' which allows you to limit who can see these cases/tickets based on your security setup. This is especially helpful for areas such as payroll or benefit questions.

You can set it up so that as a user creates new case requests, they select the case type, then it takes them through a questionnaire to capture the types of information you typically need for that type of case (i.e. a payroll question or request for a computer/badge whatever).

As someone is creating a case, based on the case type, you can show related Articles (under 'Suggested Resources') that will hopefully answer some of their questions without them even having to create a case.

You can create cases through Workday Help, Assistant, Slack/Teams, and emails.

One of the first places we are using it is to replace many of our Business Request Framework processes and move them into Case Management. This gave us better visibility (using the Help Workspace, pictured) into the requests/cases and better reporting.

Even if you have another ticketing system, you may still want to consider using the Case functionality for HR-specific requests or to replace department-specific emails like payroll@...

Leverage ETL tools your company leverages for connecting other systems for Workday as well!

July 2023

Many companies use ETL (Extract, Transform, Load) tools such as Boomi, SnapLogic, MuleSoft, Workato, or Informatica to connect their various systems together. Many also use it for Workday. Most of these tools have prebuilt connections for Workday. There is often an additional cost for these, but they could be well worth it for you.

An advantage of leveraging an ETL tool that your team already supports is that you can use the skills that your team already has, instead of them having to learn Studio. While it may not meet the needs of everything you can do with Studio, it could still be helpful and worthwhile for you to consider.

You can find an example from the Boomi website via the link at the end of this chapter.

Leverage Workday Journeys

March 2022

Workday 'Journeys' is a relatively new module that is available for purchase. The Journeys functionality includes two components:

- a tool to create a 'path' of steps to guide a worker through, which they can go through in any order

- Custom cards (cards are boxes going down the middle of the screen with the new Workday Today screen layout).

I've seen Journeys used by multiple companies to push out a set of updates and resources about COVID, as well as companies using it for significant positional changes that involve moves overseas for several years at a time. They have a Journey with 10 or so steps when they leave and another for when they return.

Use case examples for using Journeys are for specific moments of change, such as when a worker becomes a new manager, has their first child, or when someone retires. You can create a list of steps to walk staff through, some that are required while others are optional. The steps in a Journey could be:

- links to a video or website

- links to a Workday Learning course

- task links (i.e. the 'Change my home contact information' task)

- links to a document or Workday Knowledge base article (from the Workday Help Module)

A common question is- What is the difference between a BP (Business Process) and a Journey? From my standpoint, a BP is really designed for the HR staff or other 'back office' staff, whereas Journeys are created for your workers/ end users.

Journeys provides a friendly interface for staff to see all the things that could be helpful to know or do for that moment of change they are going through.

One use case that a lot of customers are talking about is transitioning the worker-oriented steps from the standard Onboarding BP to a new 'Onboarding' Journey. If you are already doing this, or are interested in discussing this, please let me know. I know of several other Workday customers interested in talking about this.

For direct links to each LinkedIn post, please visit
KeithBitikofer.com/Workday-Gold-SF-Links/